SPIRIT WALKING FOR THE RUNE MYSTIC

AN INTRODUCTION TO WORKING IN THE SPIRIT REALMS

By Frank A. Rúnaldrar

High Galdr Series
Book One: The Breath of Oðin Awakens (2nd Ed)
Book Two: The Spirit of Húnir Awakens (Part 1)
Book Three: The Spirit of Húnir Awakens (Part 2)
Book Four: The Blood of Lóðurr Awakens
Book Five: Roadmap to High Galdr Rune Work

Arts of Seidr Series
Spirit Walking for the Rune Mystic

Questions & Answers Series
The Breath of Oðin Awakens - Questions & Answers
The Spirit of Húnir Awakens - Questions & Answers

SPIRIT WALKING FOR THE RUNE MYSTIC

An Intoduction to
Working in the Spirit Realms

by
Frank A. Rúnaldrar

Part of the Arts of Seiðr Series
www.artsofseidr.com

Published in 2020 by:
Bastian & West
www.bastianwest.com

Copyright © 2020 Frank A. Rúnaldrar

The moral right of the author has been asserted.

All rights reserved. No part of this publication may be reproduced or transmitted in any form or by any means, electronic or mechanical, including photocopying, recording, or by any information storage and retrieval system, without permission in writing from the copyright holder. Reviewers may quote brief passages.

Part of the Arts of Seiðr Series
www.bastianwest.com/seidr

ISBN: 978-0-9955343-9-1

A CIP catalogue record for this book is available from the British Library.

Editor: James Millington
Cover Design: Bastian & West (internal)

Book typeset in Niva Light by PeGGO Fonts, Norse font by Joël Carrouché and runic elements in Felt-Tip Futhark by Thomas Kaeding

Copyright Notice: All rights, title and interests in the copyrights to all materials (including but not limited to any proprietary knowledge, data, information, manuals, illustrations, diagrams, flowcharts, marks or other information therein contained or thereby disclosed and representing the author's original works), are hereby reserved and to be considered the exclusive property of and belong exclusively to the author. The purchase of this book by any person(s), and its usage by any other party, shall not be construed as granting or conferring any rights by license or otherwise to the purchasing party or any other party who may come in possession of the book and/or its materials. No part of this publication or its materials may be reproduced, distributed, disseminated, or transmitted in any form or by any means and for any purpose, including but not limited to photo-copying, recording, or other electronic or mechanical methods, without the prior written permission and consent of the author, except in the case of brief quotations embodied in critical reviews and certain other non-commercial used permitted by copyright law. In the event any reader or third party submits to the author or the publisher, either jointly or severally, any questions, then any questions based on, derived from or incor-porating any of the author's materials in this publication, together with any answers provided by the author, if any, shall be deemed to be works derived from the author's copyrighted materials and accordingly such reader or third party in submitting its questions irrevocably agrees to the exclusive and royalty free world wide transfer and assignment (free of costs) of all or any rights, title or benefit in such questions to the owner for its discretionary use in any format and by any medium.

Usage Disclaimer: It is expressly agreed and acknowledged by all and any reader(s) and any parties that come into possession of the materials that all materials, information, techniques, methods, processes or statements made in this publication, and all and any associated materials as may be derived therefrom and distributed from time to time in any written or tangible forms and in any media (including electronic media), as the case may be, by the author or its publisher(s), are for to be used strictly for educational purposes only (the "Permitted Purpose") and not for any other personal or commercial purpose. All materials reflect the author's personal views and opinions, and no method or process or statement or anything else said in the materials is to be treated as having any scientific value, validity or status. Under no circumstances whatsoever or howsoever are any materials in this book, in whole or in part, intended to operate as scientifically proven methods, processes or statements, or intended to offer any medical or other advise, or be used in substitute for medical advise of and/or treatment by physicians for any matters. Neither the author nor its publisher(s) make any statement, representation, guarantee or undertaking howsoever or whatsoever as to the usefulness of any materials. The use of the materials for any other purpose, including any personal or commercial purposes other than for educational purposes, contrary to the Permitted Purpose, is not promoted and strictly prohibited. The author and its publisher(s) accept no risk, responsibility or liability for any unsanctioned use, which shall be at the user's sole risk, and shall, together and severally (the "Released and Indemnified Parties"), be held harmless and indemnified by any users engaging in any unsanctioned use contrary to this disclaimer from all and any claims, rights, liabilities, demands, obligations, conditions, promises, acts, costs, expenses, accountings, damages or actions of whatsoever kind or nature, whether in law or otherwise, whether known or unknown, which they made have or may thereafter have against the Released and Indemnified Parties for or by any reason of any occurrence, matter or thing which arise or are claimed to have arisen out of or in connection with any such unsanctioned use of the materials.

Table of Content

Spirit Walking
- Definition of Norse Terms i
- The Norse Tradition - Heritage of the Indo-Europeans .. vii
  - The Eddas vii
  - The Saga(s) x

Understanding Seiðr
- The Art of Wielding Natural Order 1
- The Völva and Seiðr 9
- So What is Seiðr? 13
- Seiðr and Men 15

Part I - Working with Spirits
- Basics of Spirit Walking 21
  - Emotionless Reality 21
  - Not All Spirits are Just Spirits 23
  - What Do Spirits Want From Humans? 24
  - What Is in It For Us? 26
  - Good, Bad, Light, Dark, Black, White, Grey Spirits? 28
  - Harmful or Helpful? 31
  - What About Evocation? 32
  - How About Invocation? 33
  - Way Forward? 34

Part II – Which Spirit?
- Selecting a Spirit Type 39
- Spirits of Midgard (Earth) 41
  - Fire 42
  - Flame 42
  - Light 43

- Air 43
- Wind 44
- Water 44
- Sea & River 45
- Earth 46
- Rock 47
- Tree 47
- Other Plants 47
- Nature 48
- Landvættir 49
- Ice 49
- Rime 50
- Snow 50
- Mist & Fog 51
- Metal 51
- Shadow 52
- Darkness 53
- Venom/Poison 53
- Creation of Spirit(s)? 55
- Final Notes for Spirit Selection 57

Part III – Connecting with Spirits

- Approaching the Spirit 61
  - Spirit (Óðr) Projection 62
  - Quantum Jumping Consciousness 67
  - Runic Trance 68
  - Harmonic Meditation 69
  - Getting Someone Else to Do It for You 70
  - Using the Name of the Spirit 72
  - Letting the Spirit Approach You 72
  - Notes for Men 73

Part IV – Building the Relationship

- Shaping the Spirit 77
  - Imposition of Form and Naming 78
  - Understanding the Spirit Type and Helping it Shape Itself 80
  - Building an Energy Body (Hamr) for the Spirit 81
- Building and Enhancing the Connection 85
  - Energy Bathing 86

ENERGY EXCHANGE 87
A PHYSICAL ANCHOR? 89

PART V – ENHANCING SPIRIT SYMBIOSIS
COMMUNICATING WITH SPIRITS 93
STEP 1 - FIRST APPROACH 94
STEP 2 - CONNECTING 95
STEP 3 - LISTENING, FEELING AND SEEING 97
STEP 4 - QUICK SYNCH 99
SPIRIT FEEDING 101
RUNIC CREATION OF SUBSTANCE 102
PULLING SUBSTANCE OUT OF THE ENVIRONMENT 103
FEEDING THE SPIRIT WITH MEGIN 106
SPIRIT GIFTING 107

PART VI – WALKING WITH SPIRITS
MERGING WITH THE SPIRIT – SHARED EXPERIENCING ... 111
GOING TO ITS NATIVE REALM(S) 117
ALLOWING THE SPIRIT TO EXPERIENCE THROUGH YOUR BODY 121
SPIRIT SEX 125
MERGING OF HVELS 132

APPENDIXES
APPENDIX A: TABLE OF RUNIC NAMES IN ICELANDIC & GERMANIC 141

APPENDIX B: REFERENCES & FOOTNOTES 145

FORTHCOMING TITLES 149

Definitions of Norse Terms

All terms used refer to their original Old Norse or Proto-Germanic meanings not their modern day derivatives in the Scandinavian, German or Icelandic languages.

Önd – Part of the psycho-spiritual construct of the Self as viewed in Norse mysticism and mythology, the Önd sits at the apex of the spiritual level of the Self and can be loosely described as 'The Breath of Oðin' or luck / Megin-fulled breath.

Óðr (or Óðr, or Óð) – Part of the psycho-spiritual Self- sitting at the apex of the mental part of the Self, it can be loosely thought of as the conscious awareness or totality of the spirit.

Hugr – The Hugr is often thought of as the reasoning or logic part of the mind, sometimes as the mind itself and often as the intellect or intellectual capacity of the mind. Essentially it is the manifestation of the active characteristics of the Spirit (Óðr).

Minni – The polar opposite of the Hugr and often thought of as the root of memory, the Minni is actually the individual record of one's experiences and acts as an anchor point for those events.

Hamr – The Hamr is the energy body, often described as the blueprint of the physical.

Lik – Part of the psycho-spiritual Self sitting at the apex of the energetic part of the Self, the Lik is the complete physical body as a result of the fusion of matter and spirit via the medium of energy. When talking about the Lik we include everything which is part of it, including the energetic and spiritual elements as well as the typically physical ones such as blood, DNA, nervous system and so forth.

Sal – Part of the psycho-spiritual self sitting at the bottom of the energetic part of the Self, the Sal is often loosely translated as the 'shadow'. In effect, it is the complimentary opposite of the Hamr.

Heimdall – One of the principle Gods in Norse mythology, Heimdall was described as the white god or whitest of the gods. He is linked to light and the pure power thereof. He possesses the resounding horn Gjallarhorn, which he will sound at the time of Ragnarök. He is the God responsible for originating the various classes of mankind and imbuing these with increasing degrees of divinity.

The Æsir – This refers to the clan of Gods from Ásgarð, typically associated with the divine aspects of spiritual origin. They are wielders of the Galdr sciences (use of runes and their correct applications) and have strong connections with the spiritual, awareness, intellect, mind, knowledge and the sciences.

The Vanir – The Vanir refers to the clan of Gods from Vanaheim, typically associated with the natural order of things and having strong connections with nature, the world and the physical as it moves towards the spiritual. They are wielders of Seidr crafts (sorcery, divination, soothsaying, shamanistic practices, herbal medicines and so forth).

Yggdrasil (Mjötvið) – The mythical Ash tree that is home to the nine worlds in Norse cosmology. It is also thought of as being the foundation of the cosmos itself and everything within it.

Egil's Saga – Otherwise termed in Iceland as the Egla, this is an Icelandic Saga dating back to 1240 AD, which details the life of Egil Skallagrimsson a farmer, Viking and poet.

Muspelheim – Muspelheim was the first world to be formed out of the great emptiness called Ginnungagap. It is a realm of flame, fires, light and explosive power unreachable by any not native to it.

Húnir (Hœnir) – One of the Æsir Gods, he helped create mankind along with Oðin and Lóðurr. He gave the first man and woman Óðr and hence imbued them with spirit. He is also one of the Gods who survives Ragnarök and gains prophetic powers thereafter.

Njörðr – Vanir god of the Sea, he is the father of Freya and Frey and was one of the hostages exchanged in the Æsir-Vanir war. It is said he will return to head the Vanir after Ragnarök.

Lóðurr (Lóð or Lóðr) – Lóðurr is a mysterious God, whom academics seem unable to accept other than trying (and failing) to identify him with Loki or even Freyr. He gives the first man and woman blood and hence health, in other words flesh or physicality.

Ragnarök – Also known as the Twilight of the Gods, this final battle was foretold in the Völuspá (stanza 41). It describes the ultimate fate of the Gods themselves.

Ætts – Meaning 'clan', it can also refer to related grouping of concepts, individuals or sets of people. It is sometimes referred to as kin-Ætts which would be used in terms of a grouping of related people. For instance, Ætts in terms of individuals would include related individually such as family, whereas kin-Ætts would expand this to a wider set of relations such as an entire clan.

Norns – This typically refers to the Jotun (giantess) sisters Urð, Verðandi and Skuld who weave the threads of fate for men and gods alike. They also draw water from the Well of Urð and collect sands from around it to pour on the Yggdrasil to prevent it from rotting. The word Norn can also refer to the concept of the fate weaver attached to individuals at birth which could be either good or bad, weaving either a fortunate or unfortunate fate for that individual.

Niflheim – One of the Nine Worlds in Norse Cosmology, Niflheim is a world of primordial ice and cold, sometimes also called the mist world.

Fylgja – Part of the archetypal level of the Self, the Fylgja is a spirit which binds to the individual, becoming a part of him or her upon birth. It is always inherited down the ancestral lines and carries experiential essence and memories and powers of the former Self's embodiment. The Fylgja forms into either animal, humanoid or geometric form depending on evolutionary progress of both the individual and itself.

Kin-Fylgja – Similar to the Fylgja, this overarching spirit carries the experiential essences of the entire family line, the sum resulting from the entire ancestral lines up to the current point. It attaches to the eldest male of the family line and communicates primarily through the females of the line.

Hamingja – The Hamingja is part of the archetypal level of the Self. It manifests as an energetic organ in the individual which stores the Megin (power) it produces from various runic and life energies.

Wyrd and Ørlǫg – This refers to fate or rather threads of fate as they flow through creation. Cosmically, Ørlǫg is seen as infinite fibres of energetic substance flowing throughout all existence. From a human perspective, these fibres appear to flow through Creation but also through individuals, Gods and all life forms, setting the path they will follow over the course of their existence. However, when viewed from a Cosmic perspective, all things in Creation flow through the fibres. The Wyrd refers to these threads on a larger scale such as for humanity as a whole, individual races and clans while Ørlǫg refers to how these threads manifest on the individual level. The Wyrd is formed by the Norns and the Ørlǫg is build from the Wyrd based on individual's power, fate and evolutionary needs by the Fylgja.

Óðrerir (Odhrærir, Óðrørir) – This refers to the container or cauldron which holds the sacred mead. Its equivalent is the legend of the 'Holy Grail' in Arthurian mythology and the 'Holy Chalice' in Christian mythology. The Óðrerir may well have been the inspiration for these later myths.

The Norse Tradition - Heritage of The Indo-Europeans

It is impossibly difficult to determine the full extent of or to search out all sources of the Norse tradition. Most pre-date the widespread availability of writing, while others were passed exclusively from one generation to the next orally. The main sources of knowledge left to us in this modern day and age are found in the Eddas and the Sagas.

The Eddas

The term 'Eddas' comes from Old Norse and it is used by modern-day students and academics to refer to two main Icelandic literary works that serve as the basis of our knowledge of Norse mythology, tradition, teachings and history.

There are two primary Eddas, both written during the 13th Century in Iceland. The first set is grouped under the label 'Poetic Eddas', which predate even the Viking Age, and come from an unknown source.

They are divided into two sections; the first is a narration of the creation, destruction and rebirth of the world and provides the mythology of the Norse deities as well. The second is a set of legends relating to Norse heroes, kings and wise men.

The Poetic Eddas were incorporated into the Codex Regius written during the 13th century. Unfortunately, it was not until the mid-1600s that the Codex resurfaced in the hands of Brynjólfur Sveinsson, a bishop to the Church of Iceland in Skálholt. Brynjólfur was also a scholar at heart, hence his fascination with the old myths and legends! It is he who collected and produced this compilation of Old Norse mythology and heroic poems into the Eddas. However, it is widely accepted that he was not their author and so they were not labelled after him. He gifted his findings to King Christian IV of Denmark in manu-script form, thus earning it the name Codex Regus, which was then preserved in the Royal Library until 1971 when a formal return was made to Iceland.

The second Eddas were compiled from traditional oral sources and (theorised to be derived from) an unknown set of Eddas often referred to as the Elder Eddas by Icelandic scholar Snorri Sturluson (dated from the 14th century). He collated these literary works under the label of Prose Eddas. Like the Poetic Eddas, the Prose Eddas also describe in detail the creation, destruction and rebirth of the world, Norse mythology and life. Due to his background and the time period in which Snorri lived, the 'Christianisation' of certain concepts and legends are to be found in this text. Nonetheless, it does provide an invaluable and rich account of the Norse tradition and, just as importantly, how it was recounted over the generations.

Scholars have long held the view that the Poetic Eddas, and therefore the Prose Eddas, came from a much older source. The rediscovery of what is known as the Elder Eddas helped confirm that suspicion. The Elder Eddas are comprised of the Pagan poems and teachings that were later hinted at in Snorri's Prose Eddas.

Many translations from Old Norse can be found and the number thereof seems to increase steadily over time. One key point to keep in mind is that the Eddas are complex literary works detailing the Norse tradition through poetry and prose. Accordingly, when reading various translations, different terms and words are often found to express the same underlying concept or similar words are used to describe totally different ones. Add to this the fact that many Old Norse terms have no equivalents in modern day languages, and it becomes vitally important to read in between the lines, so to speak, referring back to the concept rather than relying strictly on the words themselves. A literal, legalistic reading that has become completely engrained in the modern readers' minds will fail to capture the actual meanings, concepts and knowledge held within the Eddas.

Aside from those mentioned, other so-called Eddas can be found. These are typically adaptations in use by specific groups based on either the Prose or Poetic Eddas. The key point to note, however, is that those are adaptations.

The translations of the Prose and Poetic Eddas that have been used as source materials for this work can be found in both the references and further reading sections. Modern day adaptations and/or derivatives are not used.

The Saga(s)

Unlike the Eddas, the term Saga (story) refers to one of the many stories, poems, legends and so forth. Not all the Sagas made it into the Eddas. Individual Sagas might have not been discovered until a much later, post-Eddas compilation period.

These Sagas are individual tales in prose or poetic form detailing historical events of heroic deeds, tales or important persons (a great many of them Vikings, Pagans or even sometimes Christians), bishops, saints and even legendary heroes. Many of the Sagas include tales of kings, special individuals (such as the Egil Sagas used in this text), and even territorial historic events ranging from the Nordic countries to the British Isles, France and even North America (Canada in particular)[1]. Their main characteristic is that they are a historical statement or tale (that is the literal meaning of the term Saga). This has raised much speculation as the intellectual machinery attempts to digest material that is these days considered to be supernatural or metaphysical.

This range of subject matter is simply due to the fact that these records were, more often than not, kept within individual families, transmitted orally or simply brought from a different territory. Remember, the Old Norse people (Indo-Europeans) existed long before the Viking age and had to survive forced Christianisation, dispersion of territories, hostile natural environments, and so forth. In other words, these Sagas provided additional insights into the traditions, mythology, legends and teachings that were initially transmitted orally and then, once writing became widely available, were from time to time published. Even to this date, however, many of the Sagas have never been published and are kept from public view for a variety of reasons. Some of these reasons are of a very practical nature. In Iceland, for instance, these stories are considered to be part of the national heritage, hence books or manuscripts that are valued as family heirlooms, if known about, would be confiscated by the state on the basis of it being a national treasure. This is somewhat of an over-simplification but is an example of one of the many reasons why a lot of these Sagas never have (and most probably never will) see the light of public accessibility or dissemination. Others might hold deep-seated hereditary knowledge, which, more often than not, requires specific genetic and energetically transmitted capabilities to be of any use. This is the case with the higher mysteries bestowed upon the Jarls by Heimdall.

Fortunately, many Sagas are available for public consumption, and they do provide an exceptional insight into the wisdom and traditions of our ancestors. In this work, the Sagas are used to illustrate and gain further insights into teachings from older sources, be they part of the oral tradition or those in the Eddas[2].

This seeming endless diversity of sources is what makes studying the Old Norse tradition wildly exciting and fascinating beyond expectation, yet also insanely frustrating. Each Saga and Edda can expand our understanding, yet finding the relevant ones can be a most noteworthy challenge, in addition to actually understanding the knowledge therein once it is found! Nevertheless, gaining a reasonably solid foundation into the tradition is key; it is after all part of our heritage and is what empowers us. The appendices will provide more references and recommended reading. Fear not, however — all Eddas and Sagas relevant to the topics and teachings in this book have been included; for without basing such teachings in the actual texts and other sources of heritage they would hold no validity per se. It is of vital importance to work with these Eddas and Sagas as the foundation upon which we build our spiritual heritage.

UNDERSTANDING SEIÐR

THE ART OF WIELDING NATURAL ORDER

What is Seiðr? This question might be far more difficult to answer than at first it may seem. Seiðr is these days being promoted as a type of shamanism because it involves trance work and leaving the physical reality temporarily, or as a form of witchcraft, because the entire scope of manipulating elemental forces somehow, over time, seems to have been conveniently forced into that categorisation box. There is no need for us to go into deconstruction of the entire concept of what a witch was back in the old days, what one is today and so forth because in the Norse tradition, no such thing exists.

Our concept of the Völva is clearly rooted in that of the seeress and prophecy. Yes, the völur had power over nature as well, but this was typically secondary to their role as seers. It is only natural for one who sees into alternate reality to learn from what one sees. Just as today's sciences observe, experiment and then build tools to manipulate the forces (and effects thereof) of what has been observed.

The practice of Seiðr traces its roots far into the distant past. Sources within the Eddas tell us that the Goddess Freya taught it.

"Njorð´s daughter was Freya, she was a sacrificial priestess, she was the first to teach the Aesir the art of seiðr, a practice of the Vanir."[3]

We see that, Seiðr in and off itself, springs forth from the realm of the gods – the Vanir, to be precise. Did it have bite? Of course it did; remember all the forces are at war. This might come as a surprise or even a shock to the modern-day reader but it remains a universal fact. The balance and counterbalance of forces in creation is constantly in flux. That very flux represents the underlying struggle for survival and in many cases for dominance. It is a fundamental fact of creation. It is natural that Seiðr could be used to help as well as harm. That is the law of nature and, beyond that, of existence itself. The seeds of life can bloom into plants which can heal or kill.

It is also just as important not to fall in the fallacy of defining an entire tradition spanning hundreds of practices and hundreds of years, for that matter, as just shamanism, which is a more appropriate term for the American Indian practices than the Norse. Such misconceptions are very problematic and hide from view what it actually was. What Seiðr is understood to be in the modern area is an altogether different matter, because these days, more so than in the past, it is a very hidden art. What we find in the public remit is in a very limited form, and more often than not, is a remodelling of what little snippets of information from our sources are found intermixed with modern-day new age practices. Even when attempting to recreate techniques from the original written sources directly, you always face the iron-clad problem of having to fill gaps because the underlying keys to them have never been written. Due to these (and many more) factors, what most modern minds understand Seiðr as being has very little in common with the actual Seiðr practices. Additionally, like all things, it has evolved and is still changing.

When looking at the arts of Seiðr as a whole, it is important to remember that its practitioners lived in a harsher reality than we do today, and this would have had a strong impact on their practices. In the modern era, people are looking for Seiðr's power rather than its original currents and applying it to all sorts of ventures. Whether it is what we label dark or not depends now entirely on the person; a modern day Seiðr practitioner would just as likely – if not more so – use it to assist than to harm. It is important to note that we do have accounts in the Eddas and Sagas of it being used for both purposes as well, but then again, who is to say what is harmful and what is not? Accounts where a Seiðr woman would raise a tempest at sea and drown the boats of armies at war with those she sided were, from those armies' perspective, a horrific act of evil, yet from the point of view of those she protected were the greatest and most noble thing they could hope for. For them, the spirits were on their side and she was their representative in Midgard. It is all a matter of perspective.

A less confusing definition of Seiðr would be the art of wielding the forces of creation and becoming a type of mid-point for them. We can label this as sorcery for the sake of clarity. Its users walk in both Midgard and beyond. Interestingly, there are three types – or, if you prefer, branches of Seiðr. Most contemporary writers fail to grasp this basic concept even though it is not only explicitly pointed to in the Eddas themselves but is also reflected in various accounts and Seiðr practices themselves.

> "Eru völur allar
> frá Viðolfi,
> vitkar allir
> frá Vilmeiði,
> seiðberendr
> frá Svarthöfða,
> jötnar allir
> frá Ymi komnir."[4]

The number of popularised mis-translations of this stanza is staggering, in just how misrepresented the underlying meaning of this turns out to be. The most popular translates the Völva as witches, Seiðberendr as transsexuals and Seiðmennir as sorcerers (probably the best one of the three). We will look at the Völva in detail below. Let us take a brief look at the term 'vitkar', often translated as 'wizard', though in Norse Heathen societies, the meaning of 'sorcerer' is attributed to the term. A more accurate Old Norse term for those would be 'galdramað' (magician or wizard). As far as 'sorcerer' is concerned, if we disregard the modern-day perversion of the term and look back, it is not quite what it seems to be. From the Latin and Indo-European roots of the term 'sorcerer', we get 'lot', 'fate', 'to sort' and 'line-up'. All pointing towards the concept of a man ordering things in a specific pattern, which could then be termed the flow of fate (or how things unfold, based on that pattern/order). So where does that leave us with 'vitkar'? It is actually quite straightforward; 'vitkar' is the plural form of 'vitki', which in Old Norse, also means 'a wise man'. The form of wisdom referred to in this particular case is most likely one gained from exploration of the more hidden facts of life, reality and existence. Only with knowledge of all things does one gain true wisdom. The final perplexing term is 'Seiðberendr'. This is the plural of 'Seiðberandi', which can be broken down to 'spell' or 'enchantment', combined with the action of carrying or having to bear. This gives us the definition of 'Seiðberendr' being someone who is made to bear a curse or carries and enchantment. In some sources, it is also referred to as being workers of charms or spell-singers. But those arts can be found in all facets of Seiðr and are by no means exclusive to the Seiðberendr. This gives us:

> 'All the seeresses come from Viðolfi,
> All wise men from Vilmeiði,
> Curse bearers (or carriers of enchantment) from Svarthöfða and
> All Jötnar (giants) from Ymi'

Some sources go on to look at the meaning behind the names of the progenitors but this is not necessary since all that which is being referred to here is who the ultimate ancestor is – their name in particular. The importance is the name itself rather than the meaning of the name. 'Svarthöfða' can loosely be transcribed as 'Black Head', 'Viðolfi' as 'Wood-wolf' and 'Vilmeiði' as 'Wishing Tree'. The Uppland Runic Inscription of 1014 was inscribed as being raised in the memory of Svarthöfði and his sons, hinting at the fact that we are dealing with a living ancestry rather than an encapsulation of a symbolic concept. The final ancestry is that of Ymir. There are a few important points we need to take from all this. One is that Seiðr was not only practiced by women (Oðin himself being the proof of that), the second point is that the practice of Seiðr had a number of different ancestral sources and that the sex of the one practicing it is limited to the ancestry. All vitkar came from Vilmeiði, and all Völva came from Viðolfi – a direct line of ancestry based on sex of the seer(ess). Then you get the Seiðberendr, who are descendants of Svarthöfð and his sons. This might seem a little odd, but when you look at the practical side of Seiðr, it starts to make sense. The practical methods of Seiðr are, in a lot of cases, substantially different for men and women (in all Seiðr cases, sex = gender, so there is no point making any such distinctions here. It is simply due to the fact that many practices rely on energetic functions of the organs, both physical and non-physical).

There are additional terms in Old Norse which point to Seiðr users. Actually, there are so many, it would be a waste of time covering them all here. Some of the more common ones you will find are Seiðmann (Seiðr – man) and Seiðkona (Seiðr – woman). These simply refer to a man or a woman practicing Seiðr. These are good and solid terms to use in order to avoid confusion. All men and woman can learn Seiðr, whereas only those of particular ancestries can learn to be Vitkar or Völva. Unless you have the natural aptitude for seership or prophecy, there is no training to make you one. If you do, the training will amplify and direct those natural abilities. This is why the multitude of students of Seiðr who go about trying to emulate the high seat prophecies seldom have any concrete results. As for Seiðberendr those originated from an enchantment or curse. These flow in the bloodlines down the male generations. It is possible to initiate them into their full Seiðberendr birthrights as well, and to some lesser extent, some of the Seiðr sexual practices for men perform a lesser version of those. Having said all of that, leaving these specialisations to the side, Seiðr is open to anyone who seeks to follow the path of these Vanir and Jötnar arts.

The Völva and Seiðr

When looking at Seiðr, it is virtually important NOT to confuse it with the arts of the Norns and Völva. In the Norse trinity of mystical arts and sciences, you have:

Seiðr – Sorcery
Spá – Prophecy
Galdr – Rune Sciences

The Seiðr was practiced by women, Galdr by men and the Spa by either, but we more often than not have women doing so because our records of male prophecy are virtually non-existent. When we look at High Galdr, we will learn how to unleash the prophetic skills by its use rather than by the use of Seiðr. Traditionally, Spá means prophecy and a spákona was a woman who specialised as a seer. There is nothing more concrete than its manifestation in the Eddas first poem called the Völuspá – which, incidentally, is translated as the prophecy of the Völva. In the Völuspá, we see the full extent of the power of a Völva. Most readers misinterpret the passages as a memory, as if the Völva was remembering rather than seeing. This is a natural error which derives from a lack of understanding how seership functions. When she describes herself as remembering, it is no longer the Völva who is talking. Rather, her awareness has by that point expanded and merged with the underlying awareness of creation. She is speaking from ITS perspective, not her own. Her words should be read as an account of that infinitely vast awareness which spans through everything. That awareness does indeed remember a time before time itself. It is a given that it would, because it was there at the seeding of creation herself. Once this knowledge is taken into account, the rest of the stanzas make perfect sense, and it illustrates how this ability works perfectly.

> "...that I remember from longest ago."[5]

> "I remember jǫtuns
> born long ago,
> those who once me
> had nurtured;
> nine worlds I remember,
> nine giantesses inside,
> the great mjötvið (world tree)
> down under the ground."[6]

Here, the Völva having merged with this ancient primal awareness talks of how it remembers a distant past when the Jǫtuns (giants, children of Ymir) nourished or nurtured her. The Norse uses the feminine term in relation to the nurturing for good reason. It speaks of the very nature of this primal awareness. We will not delve into that at this point; it would take us too far off-topic. This awareness remembers the planting of the World Tree, remembers it in its seedling stage. It also recalls the nine giantesses within it. This might be confusing to those unfamiliar with Norse mythology but the worlds themselves were considered giantesses and often referred to as such. For instance, Thor's mother Hlôdyn (also called Jörð), the personification of the Earth itself (Midgard), is considered to be both a giantess and in some cases, a goddess too. Likewise, the other eight worlds were likewise giantesses in their own right. This of course is not referring to actual giants but the planet's essence. It is very simple to think of it in terms of the actual planet being the physical body and the giantess personification being the energy or spirit of the planet or world. Here, she tells us how these nine giantesses are in the wood of Mjötvið (Yggdrasil).

For those of you who think foresight and prophecy is nonsense in its own right, it is worth noting that it was recognised and commented on in the modern-day sciences. The psychiatrist and neurologist Arthur Deikman describes the phenomenon as an 'intuitive knowing, a type of perception that bypasses the usual sensory channels and rational intellect'[7].

Having said all this it is important to keep in mind that unlike with Seiðr and Galdr, which you could learn, with Spá mysteries it was not possible without the underlying natural ability or aptitude for it. You either had the inherent ability or you did not. It mattered little how much you practised or what you did – the very ability had to be there and when it was, then the relevant training was undertaken to nurture and grow it. Because most (if not all) of the Völva were both spákona (seeresses) and seiðkona (Seiðr women), the two would blend into each other rather readily, due to this Seiðr and Spá become more and more intertwined at a higher level of practice. Being a Völva (a seeress) was an altogether different matter than being a Seiðr woman. The Völva were born, and they are the representatives of the Norn races across the Nine Worlds, and they had quite a distinction in society (the high seat was always offered to the Völva by the lords of the lands she would visit as a sign of respect), whereas the Seiðr women of power were feared, but there, the respect was one more akin to fearful respect. The latter represented power; the former knowledge and pre-cognition. The former would wield powers to shift and counter the flow of fate, whereas the latter were its ultimate representatives. Seiðr was, as a matter of tradition, taught to all women, to a certain degree. The basics were expected to be known to them all.

So What is Seiðr?

Think of it as a collection of practices, which unlock the human potential at the non-physical level, which then allow its wielder to manipulate both the physical and those non-physical realities.

Is it shamanism? No: sticking Seiðr into the box called shamanism is like taking one finger on your hand and saying it is the entire hand. Seiðr is vast, powerful, raw and dangerous. It comes in many forms and is adopted in many ways. What we are going to look at in these teachings are some of the more mysterious (and hence hidden) parts of this art as it was taught from mother to daughter (and, on very rare occasions, sons) throughout the ages. Some of you might wonder why the term 'art' is used when referring to Seiðr. Unlike Galdr, Seiðr cannot be practiced along the scientific mindset. It does have methods, but those are far from the very precise formulistic ones available to Galdr. In this case, the practices are broad and adaptable (providing you keep the key requirement elements). They can be personalised. They require a certain degree of self-understanding and ability to be intuitive as well as creative. When practicing the arts of Seiðr, the results can be unpredictable. Depending on your skills, they will vary and they might manifest in different ways. Here, your personal power and experience will have a very significant impact on your Seiðr. Everything is more fluid, less concrete and tends to follow energetic patterns. The subjective elements of our minds have a far greater impact on all outcomes than do the objective ones. Additionally, ancestral influences do make their mark far more prominently. Weaving all of these elements together, alongside your knowledge of energy and the nine realms, is an essential for Seiðr. For this reason, it is best to think of it as an art form – unlike Galdr, where you have put together a precise set of runes to achieve a specific outcome in a specific situation.

Women will find it incredibly intuitive, natural and free flowing; men will have to work harder at this, much harder.

 Seiðr and Men

This was one of the most controversial subjects at the time. There were countless debates taking place over whether Seiðr was or should be practised by men. In Germanic tradition, it was mainly practised by women. Most notably because it was deemed 'unmanly' (with a few exceptions: notably, the berserker trance warrior practices which were also a form of Seiðr). It was during ancient times, when it was the role of men to be warriors, not stay back at home and dabble in the mysteries. The other reason for this was most likely due to the fact that Seiðr required an intuitive mindset rather than a logic or reason-based one. This was generally seen as being more of a masculine mode of thinking than the intuitive and feeling-based mindset which was thought of as feminine. Women, on the other hand, were at a great advantage: their natural perceptual abilities would always trump those of a man, and they still do to this very day. Energetic reality and physical reality were both the same thing for them: one reality – well, until the advent of Christianity, in any case. Practicing Seiðr was just as natural as it was for the men to go out into battle. Speaking traditionally, it was seen as the duty of every mother to teach her daughters the songs and poems of the old, which were used to unlock the flow of Seiðr power. Those of you who have made a closer reading of the Eddas and Sagas will find references to this when the Völva ask if any of the women know (or remember) the poems of their foremothers.

The lesser-known drivers of this gender-based division was that there were, in fact, a set of practices which were for biological reasons, outside of the scope of men's ability to practice. Men did not possess a womb and were lacking the unique abilities provided by the energetic functions of this organ which were required for many Seiðr practices. Yes, the deep mysteries of these arts were based around the harnessing of sexual energies. However, there were also Seiðr practices which were catered for men's sexuality. Other variations of Seiðr, although not generally excluding men, were far more dangerous for men to practice than for women. Remember, most of creation is feminine in its nature; the male energy type in extremely precious and, energetically speaking, a very coveted commodity. Additional differences in the Hamr and in the shadow (Sal) structures made it exceptionally challenging for men to practice. We will not delve into those differences here.

These were general rules, and there were men who did embark upon the practice of these arts. One of the most well known was none other than Oðin himself. Once he mastered them, his powers became a legend in their own right – although if you read the Eddas closely, you will see that they were somewhat different from those of the Völva, whom he consulted with on a regular basis to make up for his shortcomings. In other places such as Iceland, Seiðr was more often practiced by men than women. The inversion was so dominant that records of murdered 'witches' in Iceland point to the fact that far more men were killed for its practice than women[8].

In Finland, their sorcerers were relied upon for the healing and protection of the men and women of their tribes. In connected traditions, such as the druidism of the Celts, the druids were all men, due to the ancient knowledge that nature was actually masculine and not the inversion of what is promoted today amongst the new-age beliefs of a 'Mother Nature'. Earth was the mother, while nature and the seas were the father elements, just as the sun (Sól) was feminine and the moon (Máni) masculine.

In other circumstances, it was taught to men but only in rare circumstances, one of those being when a woman had no daughters but only son(s). Some mothers would, in those cases as Seiðr practitioners, pass their secrets onto a son (usually the youngest) to ensure her art and tradition did not die out. The other big exception was for bisexual men. In those days, it was held that there were no exclusively 'gay' men, since all men were expected to have a family and seed the next generation, irrespective of sexual preference. Only if they did were they free of the social stigma and had they proved not to be 'ergi' (emasculated or effeminate men) and they could delve into some of the practices of Seiðr.

Other instances of Seiðr practices amongst priests and gods occurred regularly. These were the men of mysteries. It is also interesting to note that in the then social norms, it was considered that as a man entered old age, he would become ergi (effeminate).

Naturally, these days, none of those stigmas matter. They have, for all intents and purposes, become socially outdated and irrelevant. However, the types of Seiðr accessible to men and women still present a strong gender divide – sexual Seiðr in particular, as well as certain practices which have different methodologies for men and women due to their biological differences and Hamr structural differences. Those, unfortunately, are fixed. It is all best approached with a respect for one's own strengths and weaknesses. When the need arises, we rely on the opposite sex to supplement our weaknesses and use our own strengths to support them in theirs. Much could be said on this topic but ultimately, it would be nothing more than a distraction. After all, these books are intended to focus on the practical side of things. We will leave the study of past mind-sets and social acceptability to those who are interested in these matters.

PART I – WORKING WITH SPIRITS

The Basics of Spirit Work

It is important to look at this entire topic with a strong will and objective mindset. Why this warning? Because when dealing with spirit matters, it is very easy to fall prey to one's own wishes, imagination and illusions. It is a highly subjective practice. Remember from our work in *The Spirit of Húnir Awakens* and *The Blood of Loðurr Awakens*, the spirit and mental parts of reality are entirely subjective, whereas the energetic are objective. That is the nature of the things we are dealing with. This does not mean that they are entirely so – in other words, there are objective characteristics in operation on the spiritual and mental sides of reality but the way we perceive and interact with them are highly (if not entirely) subjective.

Emotionless Reality

When dealing with the nature of spirits (Vættir), this subjectivity in perception and interaction can become a big problem if one is not constantly vigilant or if one lacks the emotional detachment needed. Remember, at this level of creation, there is no emotion yet. It is only once you manifest downwards from this level that emotion comes into existence and play. Emotion in and of itself is probably the wrong term to use, but it is the most understandable to our awareness. In actuality, feelings would be a better term since emotions are, technically speaking, products of our biological chemistry which spirits do not possess. Hence they are incapable of emotion.

This is one of the most worrisome pitfalls so commonly fallen for when people go looking for spirits. They seek out 'friends', 'lovers', 'partners' and so forth, which they fail to find in life, without understanding that a spirit is incapable of those types of relationship with anyone. The closest one can reach with a spirit is companionship, and that will last for as long as there is a need on that spirit's end. Without an energy body, a spirit is completely and utterly incapable of anything even resembling emotion. Those of you who have worked through *The Spirit of Húnir Awakens* will know that there is no emotional context in spirit work, and to achieve actual success, you will have had to separate your emotional part of the Self from the Óðr, Hugr and Minni in order to make progress. At this level, even the sense of feeling had to be pruned of the human emotional hue it typically has in order to grasp Spirit sensing as the sixth sense, so that it can start gaining the abilities to read and gain information from energy itself.

Not All Spirits are Just Spirits

This is easy to understand but difficult to perceive without fully developed spiritual senses. From a human perspective, we typically think of anything not physical as spirit, and even ghosts (which are nothing more than discarded parts of the Self) are thought of as spirits. However, this is an all-too-often highly limited interpretation of the wider scope of reality. Spirits are inherently a part of every Self in existence, but not the only part. Hence, when connecting with a spirit, you could be connecting to the spirit of a being which has a Hamr, a Lik of some sort or other, a Sal and so forth. For instance, let us take a tree: it is a living being, and its Lik (think of it as shape, if you prefer) hosts a highly complex energy system and body, which in turn is infused with a spirit. It could just as readily be a tree which existed a long time ago but no longer does. Remember when working in spirit realms time does not exist (or does not flow as it does for us). In that case, it could still have a Hamr which is still infused with its spirit, or that the Hamr could have decayed, leaving it with only a spirit. Creation is filled with all sorts of possibilities – countless ones. As a side note, the fae are what we humans usually perceive as spirits of trees, plants and other such natural life forms. They typically return to the over-arching flow of nature which we call 'Mother Nature' or 'the Spirit of Nature' or 'Gaia'. Other fae and fairies do the same but come from the real of Vanaheim or Svartelfheim instead. Interestingly, in the other worlds, we do not find fae as such, but other beings which carry out the same (or similar) functions.

Without going too far off course, it is important to keep in mind that what one is dealing with is not always 'just a spirit' but can actually be much more than just that. However, all initial dealings are done via the mental level of reality – hence all the rules of spirit reality apply. These are very fine and subtle distinctions but ones which need to be grasped if one is not to get into a whole host of difficulties later on. All too many who seek interaction with beings of the non-physical fall into countless 'traps', simply due to misunderstanding how the greater reality of creation functions, or whose spiritual development is insufficient for such complex and intricate interactions. Dealing with a 'spirit' is like dealing with an enemy, friend, child, parent and boss all rolled into one. You need to be able to function at its level or it will end up using you; that is what they do, irrespective of what they may make you believe they want. What they want is your connection to the objective realities which they lack and all the things which flow from that.

What Do Spirits Want From Humans?

This is surprisingly simple to answer: evolution. To most, this very answer will seem extremely odd, to say the least. Most of you will think that because a spirit is a spirit, it would be automatically more evolved than a human being. This is a misconception, for it could be, but it might just as well not be. The reason a spirit would seek out a human for its evolution is easy to understand once we put things into the context of the spiritual realities (the mental level of creation). In *The Spirit of Húnir Awakens*, we have looked at these rules. 'Like attracts like' being one of the key principles which apply. This is both a boon and a restriction for any spirit, as what it means is that it can only interact with other beings which are like it. Hence the breadth and scope of energy, experience and action are limited to whatever is like it. For that spirit and its consciousness to perceive or conceive of anything which is significantly different from itself, it needs to do so through the energetic level of reality, with the physical giving the broadest scope of experiencing of things which is not like itself. This is one of the big reasons why all spirit(s) seek out physical matter; by embodying themselves into matter and becoming physical, they can expose themselves to experiences which they would never be able to otherwise, because it might all be so unlike them that they will never be able to reach them or interact with them. Additionally, physicality gives them awareness. Unless a spirit has existed in flesh or a fully formed Hamr, it will not possess awareness but be limited to consciousness only (generally speaking). Most humans do not appreciate just how important matter actually is to creation. That is a hard and harsh lesson for most of us to learn, and even harder to accept, for some of us.

We have looked at the cycles of life and why what people call 'bad', 'horrible' or 'evil' things happen in life. This also works in this context (universal principles apply to all, irrespective of all other things), where such embodiment in matter does also allow the Spirit to experience the unpleasant side of things, but it does so irrespective, because those experiences also widen its scope of 'like-ness', which in turn, will expand their experiential or existential scope of the spiritual itself.

By working with a human, spirits which are not fused with flesh can also expand their scope of Self. Part and parcel of this process is living with and through the selected mystic, Seiðr man/woman, companion and so forth. Other spirits do so through consumption of the human's energy and memories, while still others do so by widening the senses of that human being and 'inviting' them into their own realm and trying to bind them there (dwarfs and fae are notorious for this). Those will then gain an extension of their realm through that human being into ours. There are many ways to achieve a diversification of scope of 'like-ness' as there are spirits.

As you might wonder, this can be both beneficial and highly detrimental. This is why this was typically, in the past, kept both secret and hidden – not in pursuance of any conspiracy theory or gatekeeping, as it is often termed these days, but due to the potential harm one can self-inflict. It was only after maturation of the spirit (Óðr), the senses and the acquisition of a certain degree of evolutionary maturity that students were introduced to spirit working. Unfortunately, for better or worse, this has all spilt into the public domain without the safeguards and teachings which would have been a pre-requisite for this type of spiritual work. It is in an effort to remedy some of that lack that this work has been put together. It is hoped that with the wisdom and knowledge which went hand in hand with the spirits, a more beneficial interaction in this Seiðr domain can be achieved by those interested in it.

What Is in It For Us?

Just as the spirit can gain certain benefits from interaction with humans, the reverse is true as well. As mentioned above, love, friendships, companionship and all that emotional based interaction is nothing more than illusory when dealing with them. That is not why you would choose to walk this path. Spirits are not there to satisfy one's base desires or fill the gap of our inability to form relationships with other human beings. Instead, the acquisition of knowledge, power, experiences and adding new layers of 'like-ness' to your own spirit, as well as awakening dormant ones, would be the aim. A spirit is very much a type of guide with whom you share a deeper (not emotional!) connection than you would with a simple guide. You are sharing part of your Self with it. This is unavoidable since even your memories or your individual experiences are part of your Self. In exchange, they do the same.

When dealing with them from our human perspective, it is extremely important for us to realise that these are impersonal powers (that is what a spirit ultimately is). It is only when we add our own biases and perceptions onto our interactions with them that we personalise them and so open ourselves up to manipulation.

Because the very thing which pulls them towards us is our capacity for awareness, especially when it starts to fully awaken, they partake in that. This (let us call it) activated awareness produces a totally unique energy in creation, which calls out to them like a sonar pulse. This is one of the main reasons why children tend to attract them, like a flame pulling in moths at night. It is childrens' pure unrestricted awareness which draws them in. This is also why, as your awareness fades, their connection and presence to you will also fade, as you are no longer of sufficient interest to them. Harsh, is it not? Well, that is how it works; who said life was nice and fair? No such thing. Reality is a harsh mistress; deal with it. Those who do not fall into delusions of emotional bonds will not care much for a spirit to fade out of their lives. The wise will accept that they have gained whatever they needed, just as the spirits will have, and they part company, making room for new companions along the path of wisdom and life. The only time this does not happen is in one of two cases: when you become bound to them for eternity in their realm, or they become so bound in you. All other interactions are purely temporary. In both these types of bindings, the bound party loses part of their Self and fills that gap with the binding. This is why it is eternal; the dependency is total and absolute. In some cases, it is the only way to go, but as long as there are other options, it would mean giving all of those up and capping one's evolution to that which you are bound to. We will not be looking at this in much detail. The path of the Rune Mystic takes us to far too great spiritual heights for us to consider such options.

Good, Bad, Light, Dark, Black, White, Grey Spirits?

This is for the benefit of those who did not read the language section in *The Spirit of Húnir Awakens (Part 1)*. When trying to categorise spirits or their nature (which, incidentally, is not categorizable by any stretch of the imagination), people have the tendency of attaching these nonsensical labels to them – more often than not, even going into extensive arguments about which is the appropriate label and how a spirit of one label cannot do something which belongs to the scope of a spirit of another label. As discussed previously, this is a matter of linguistics and the limited scope of human perceptions. Are there spirits which work with those energies? Absolutely; that would be part of their 'individual' characteristics, but that does not make them dark, grey, white or any other such thing. They are just spirits of a certain type. These classifications of light vs dark, good vs bad and in-betweens are just our ways of trying to understand things but are irrelevant as soon as you take the human limitations in perception and mind out of the picture.

But there is a distinction in the energy types all spirits manifest, use or interact with and how we perceive those. This is where you encounter an infinite multitude of variety. Because it is infinite in nature, attaching any type of label to it will simply limit our perception and scope of understanding of that being. Yes, some will have functional tendencies towards the negative and others towards the positive. They will manifest those types of energies and influences, but to call them good or evil is showing signs of lacking spiritual maturity since those very terms are human judgements imposed upon our limited perceptions of a said spirit or being. Besides that, due to the infinite variety of types of spirits, in order to even get close to categorising any spirit even remotely correctly, one would have to put aside all our human social conditioning, all our perceptual experiences and all the limitations of our lack of growth, and assume that we have reached a state of perfection. When you have achieved all those, you could get close to a remotely accurate description based on your perceptions of a spirit, but at the same time, you would not even bother with such nonsense in the first place. See the conundrum?

In the meantime, since human beings are so reliant on categorisation, you can limit this incorrect labelling by simply thinking of things in a negative and positive way. But do keep in mind that even these are subjective judgements. Unfortunately, at this stage of development, we have nothing else to use.

In the same manner, you need to be careful to iron out the perceptive errors we are all conditioned with. The most notable is that there are 'angels' and 'demons' out there trying to help or harm. In effect, there are no such things; what are called angels are nothing more than beings which appear to be made of light, and demons are beings which appear to be made out of darkness. The social tendencies dictate that anything unexplained which harms is given the demon label and those things which are unseen or unexplained which help are given the label of angels. The exact nature of these beings could be anything in creation, unless one is able to actually see them and by the same hand see, without falling to their projected illusions, that one is unable to accurately describe them. For instance, a harmful spirit can see what you would perceive as a helpful one. Say it finds that you are a strong believer in angelic (nonsense) guidance, that being will take on the appearance and energetic pattern of an angelic being and seek to gain access to you. For a rune mystic who has developed his or her powers and perceptions, the illusion is seen through immediately. Typically, those types of spirits do not even bother with such illusions when dealing with highly advanced human beings.

In other words, avoid attaching labels, categorising beings or falling prey to your wishes, whims and desires when dealing with the spiritual reality, or you will run the risk of being badly burnt by any spirit. This is the reason why we train our senses and grow our own spirit before embarking on this type of work, or we do so under the guidance of someone who is experienced in these matters.

Just to clarify, in this work, we are going to use the traditional categories but only insofar as they match their characteristics, and not as overarching labels. In other words, when looking at other living beings in the Nine Worlds, certain characteristics are prevalent in traditional texts and teachings. For instance, to describe the spirit of a dwarf as dark with dark or black skin, earthly and solid would be correct use of those terms. To describe it as dark, black and evil as a spirit would be incorrect. In the first use, we are describing its characteristics, while in the second, the attempt is to categorise the spirit itself. It is advisable to keep this important distinction in mind when reading this text.

Harmful or Helpful?

The above discussion will leave some of you confused. If things cannot be categorised as good or bad, evil or good, black or white and so forth, you might wonder how you can determine what can potentially be harmful and what you can consider safe. The reality is that all things can be both harmful and helpful, and this can even flip from the one to the other, based purely on circumstances. It is exactly the same principle as when dealing with people in general. Some might help you, others might harm you, some might be friends and turn against you, whilst others might be enemies yet given the correct circumstances, might prove to be your allies.

It is a socially imposed fallacy that there are beings which are always helpful or good or will do what is in your best interest, no matter what. They simply do not exist. Some might act in that fashion but only because it fits in with their own purposes. The moment that fit is no longer present, the situation will change – drastically so. It is a fundamental principle of reality which enables evolution to take place. Without it, evolution would not be possible and the whole point of creation would not exist either. In other words, in Old Norse conceptualisation, it would be a path to direct stasis and then back to the Ginnungagap.

This is simply the cold hard reality and it is with that knowledge that we arm ourselves and go forth into the battle for our own evolution! That is the way of the warrior – in this case, the spiritual warrior. An interesting side-note here is that the warriors were considered to be the pinnacle of the Norse trinity; they were the rulers of the clans: not kings, priests or any other; it is the warriors. Some were warriors in Midgard, others were warriors in Asgard, others warriors in Vanaheim, some destroyed entire kingdoms, others created them, and so forth – but warriors they were.

What About Evocation?

Evocation is a ceremonial way in which spirits of various sorts are made to materialise into solid form on the physical level of the energetic realities. We will not delve into this much since it has never been part of the Norse tradition itself.

The entire practice is highly complex and serves no actual purpose. One can just as effectively travel to the domain of a given spirit and interact with it there. Pulling it over here requires holes to be punctured in the gates of Midgard, which has resulted in the spiritual mess we are in today, by deliberate misuse of evocation or the accidental/unintended consequences of evocations which were not controlled. Furthermore, the power required to manifest a spirit has to be provided by the one carrying out the ritual – as well as the power to consolidate all the required effects too. Such vast expenditure of energy could be put to much better use elsewhere, and the same effects can be achieved by High Galdr or the Seiðr crafts used by oneself. Always keep in mind that everything comes at a price: the principles of X Gjöf (Gebo) always apply, irrespective of whether you want them to or not, and irrespective of you knowing about them or not.

One final note is worth making on this topic: there are not such things as lower or greater spirits. Typically, you would be instructed to use evocation for lesser or lower ones and invocation for higher or greater ones. There is no such distinction; all spirits are what they are, and this type of classification is entirely pointless in its own right.

How About Invocation?

The distinction in between evocation and invocation is that with the latter, the goal is to materialise the spirit physical as a separate entity, while with the former, the opposite is true. Here the spirit manifests within the one doing the invocation. Typically, this is reserved for the gods, where one tries to invoke them into one's Self. Unfortunately, in order to perform an actual invocation and become a true vessel for that deity, you would have to live as it would, and surround yourself in all the things which have an energetic sameness or like-ness to that spirit. The typical chanting of a quick series of words or performing a certain ceremony does nothing more than bring you into a similar energy frequency to the spirit. For an actual invocation, you need to go much deeper over a very long period of time, until the distinction between you and that spirit (or god) becomes so blurred that you can easily lose the concept of your Self and truly act as the god or goddess would, do only the things they would do, think only as they would think, behave only as they would and so forth. Such a venture takes months to execute effectively and is, for all intents and purposes, impractical to the modern man.

Having said all of that, it is possible to achieve a temporary invocation, but this only works with universal beings. Spirits who span the whole of creation can then themselves adapt to the one trying to invoke them, at the same time as that person tries to embody them. The two are then brought into synchronicity and a perfect merge occurs. Needless to say, very few spirits involve themselves in such a feat; even most of the gods would desist from doing so. We will look at a method to achieve this goal in the practical sections below.

Way Forward?

Well, with all this doom and gloom out of the way, let us move onto looking at how we can proceed forward. What we are going to delve into here is how the Seiðr practitioners interacted with spirits in general and with the spirits of inhabitants of the Nine Worlds – well, eight worlds, to be more precise. Since Muspelheim is not accessible by any being other than a native one from there, we simply cannot cover it directly, hence there is only actual access to eight of them. Oddly enough, eight is the number of spirit, unity and growth through social interactions in runic numerology. Rather appropriate.

There are a number of interesting ways of moving forward in our adventures with spirits and just as many ways of achieving various goals with this art. It is strongly recommended to have at least covered the materials in *The Breath of Oðin Awakens*, *The Spirit of Húnir Awakens* and *The Blood of Loðurr Awakens* before jumping into the practical side of this art. Those three titles (and related books) will give you the foundational skills you will be using here and the general background understanding needed. If you do not understand what is meant by making Megin flow through your arms into your spirit, you will struggle to keep up with the practices in here. If you are not able to shift into your Spirit (Óðr) to listen to or feel the spirit you are working with, you will facilitate self-deception and wishful illusions and if you cannot awaken or work with your biological intelligence or unleash Intent, you will not get far in your interactions with the spirit. Those are your basic skills. Assuming you have those tools at your disposal, the practices in here should flow without too much hindrance and you will not lose any time in attempts to weed yourself out of delusions, but instead, work practically to the most effective of your abilities.

    Remember, at all times, the spirit's scope of influence is always limited to your scope of influence. The greater your scope becomes, the more its own will widen, or it will get replaced by a spirit with a greater scope. Do not form attachments; those will just hold you back and ultimately defeat your attempts at further evolutionary progress.

    There are a few ways to approach this work. As end goals, we will look at gaining as much out of the spirits as we can in order to enhance our evolution, growth and scope of powers, boost our knowledge and hopefully, build a couple of good solid allies in the process. Ultimately speaking, the pinnacle of our work here is to enhance the scope of our Óðr and our spirits. This is a highly transformative undertaking: you will change in subtle ways, but ultimately, even with subtle changes, once they start flowing in greater numbers and at greater speed, they will start to manifest as more and more substantial changes. Always be on the lookout and self-analytical to ensure you are changing in a direction which flows with your purpose and goals. Always.

PART II – WHICH SPIRIT?

Selecting a Spirit Type

Certain people have certain affinities; actually, to be more precise, we all do. Depending on our energy types, we will be a better fit with certain types of spirits and certain entities than with others. It is pretty much the same as the social selection of friends: some people we get on with instantly, others are more work and others yet are an instant dislike. This too is due to energetic compatibility. However, on the physical side, we can seek out totally new ones, whereas on the spirit side of reality, we seek out what is closer in 'like-ness' to either what we lack, what is dormant within or what dominant energy type we are projecting outwards.

Whatever the case may be, in any of these cases, you will notice a strong pull toward a certain type of spirit. Should you have such a connection, all you really need to do is spend a little time in quiet contemplation and willing it to surface. If you do not have one, worry not; you will be able to select a spirit type you want to work with in order to enhance certain abilities or gain access to a new reality, world or energy. We will look at the general types of spirits and beings found in our tradition, which should provide more than sufficient inspiration.

Spirits of Midgard (Earth)

Having looked at how like-ness effects spirit selection in a broad context, it is time to look at some of the types of spirits you might consider working with. Naturally, those living in Midgard are the most accessible for human beings since they share the same locality of space with us. These are the elemental spirits composed of exclusively one or another element. They are the Midgard counterparts of the primal cosmic essences which gave rise to manifestation. Some of these are only accessible via Midgard due to its nature and function as the central point in Yggdrasil. Hence we find spirits of fire and flame, spirits of air and winds, spirits of water and seas, spirits of earth and rock, spirits of ice and frost, mist and shadow spirits and more. These manifestations of primal forces in Midgard are important for us to connect with and master, for they can and will unlock abilities within us which are subject to those forces. They also present us with the opportunity to touch upon forces which are not available in some of the other worlds. For instance, fire spirits are only directly accessible in Muspelheim and Midgard, ice spirits in Niflheim and Midgard and so forth.

Let us have a quick look at each of these major spirit types. In Norse (and Germanic) we use the term Vættir to denote all supernatural beings (including spirits):

Fire – These spirits represent the nuclear principle in Midgard. They are hyper active, activating and in constant, very rapid movement. Some are so fast that they dart from spot to spot without any will to do so. Unlike what most people think, they take the shapes of pure sparks, ranging from dim sparks to almost mini-suns, pulsating outwards in intense bursts. Probably some of the hardest spirits to work with, because they are such nuclei of energy and constantly hyper-activating, they can and do tire you out. Very few can withstand the presence of a high-level fire spirit. When they are forced into forms, they typically prefer male forms. No matter what form you try to contain it in, it will de-synchronise from it (separate from the form) or fracture it and then re-synchronise and rebuild it. They cannot completely be contained.

Flame – These spirits are much easier to work with than their fire counterparts. It is highly advisable to opt for a flame spirit rather than a pure fire one. Because flame is a manifestation of the characteristics of flame in Midgard (Earth), it can be contained within form much easier than pure fire. They have similar characteristics to the fire spirits but are ever so slightly slower and rather than manifesting in pure fire energy, they do so through flames. Like their fire counterparts, they manifest easier in male forms than female ones and find the former more synchronised with their nature. Flame spirits produce a lot of heat and can be extremely clingy; they too are highly activating and should be handled sparingly rather than on a regular basis because they will burn you out.

Light – Light is an important part of our lives, from sunlight or daylight all the way down to electric lights which illuminate our world at night, down to lights used in medical and production contexts, or light as an information carrier. This essence of light can be worked with in the form of a spirit. What type of level of light you work with will determine the flavour of the type of spirit connected with it. Light spirits are usually very fast, and they have a tendency of vibrating across space and more often than not, leave a buzz along your body if you are sensitive to such things. Do not make the mistake of assuming that light is always good or helpful — quite the contrary. Assumptions have to be left behind when engaging in this type of work. Look within yourself: if you see that you even might be subject to such assumptions, stay away from these spirit types (that includes light dark and shadow spirits), otherwise you will end up doing great harm to yourself. You have been warned. As for what a light spirit can provide, their realm of influence is power, as in actual force (rather than ability): they energise and can heal or harm. They ability to sharpen the mind, make one see and increase the base activity of one's abilities or atomic structures in our bodies is unparalleled. Their scope of influence is extremely rapid, very precise and to the point but also very short lived. They do not linger. They are a 'come over, do the job assigned and leave' type of spirit. This is why most of the modern day so-called 'light workers' end up falling prey to being manipulated by forms created out of their own desires. Light spirits do not linger about, keep an eye on you or play friendly. They are in constant movement and they do not linger.

Air – These spirits are extremely delicate, and flow with incredible grace and suppleness in their movements.

Gliding and flowing are good terms to use when trying to capture their motion. They too can be very active, yet rather than exploding left right and centre, they instead glide rapidly from spot to spot. They are very elusive and hard to connect with. For some reason they all have a deep bitter dislike of humans. The forms they adopt are highly etheric in appearance and have delicate features, irrespective of the gender of manifestation. Their impact on the human spirit and its capabilities is without equal. They are used to boost inspiration, communication, liberation, travel and all intellectual faculties. They have extremely good skills to boost the functions of the Hugr (mind), and Minni (memory) as well as your work on the mental level of Midgard's reality.

Wind – Wind spirits are similar to their air counterparts. However, they are far more aggressive in nature; their gliding is actually more of a type of rapid flow toward their target and a sudden burst of energy upon arrival. Think of a sonic wave hitting a target and you will get extremely close to understanding how they move. They are not pleasant spirits to work with, unless you are accustomed to them. However, they are excellent in terms of carrying messages and energies, whispering secrets and breaking free of fetters. They are excellent when a need to carry away or bring forth many things at once, such as clearing out all unwanted things in one's life. They are the muses which cause burst of inspiration. These spirits, very much as the wind itself, prefer to interact with women than men, even though the forms they take are typically male.

Water – There are essentially two types of water spirits. One could classify them as 'clear water' spirits and 'static water' spirits. In actuality, it is more of a distinction in characteristic rather than one of spirit type. Water is a tricky element: flowing, stable, inversing, life carrying, life giving and essentially energetic to its very core. It is typically the melted ice (or rime) from Niflheim, activated by heat from Muspelheim. Hence the male polarity rules it, even though it is essentially also feminine. In fact, water is both: due to its reflectiveness, it can switch but only to a certain extent. The less activity within the water, the more towards the feminine it moves, and the more activity, the greater the masculine is expressed. Since water is heavily influenced and influences the energetic and the emotional, our perceptions of it will be heavily influenced by what it reflects from within us. Those in harmony will see it as wonderful, and filled with a multitude of possibilities, while those with a darker or hateful nature will see it as more stale and foreboding. How we interpret the water's energies will also be influenced by our mastery of its powers and understanding of its nature. This is why some see the typical folklore mermaid, whilst others see delicate beings of contained bluish-green (or greenish-blue) energy in humanoid forms. In Norse, the Vatnavættir are spirits which guard specific bodies of water. Important lakes, ponds, rivers or even wells

Sea & River – Seas and rivers and their spirits are usually male, with Njörð being the god of the seas according to the Norse tradition and Poseidon according to the Greek. These are both flowing waters or raging ones of ferocious power. They represent the aggressive nature of the masculine powerhouse of Midgard (Earth). These spirits, rather than reflective, are enabling: they will serve to carry away opposition, bring forth the new and are extremely creative – often so much that they will manifest the rushes of creation which we all experience, where no matter what we need to get all this or that done, it is as if existence itself was dependent on it all being done in that very instant. Overriding drive is a key characteristic of their nature and since they are water based with strong activity, they have all the power and drive needed within themselves to achieve this without recourse to any external resources or spirits. These spirits (particularly the sea spirits: Sjóvættir), unlike their pure water counterparts, are highly active on the waking and trance parts of our consciousness. The pure water ones, on the other hand, are very active in the dream consciousness and biological awareness side of things (the body is, after all, overwhelmingly water!).

Some might wonder what about ponds? Or lakes? After all, the Lady of the Lake featured highly in Arthurian mythology. The answer is simple: a pool or lake is a large body of static water! Non-flowing water belongs to the scope of the feminine, which is why she manifested in lakes rather than rivers or the sea.

Earth – When we talk about spirits of the earth, most will think of dwarfs. This is quite appropriate, as dwarfs embody most, if not all of the characteristics of what an earth spirit would be. However, we need to be careful not to confuse them with actual dwarfs, which were born out of Ymir. They do share a lot of similarities and one could think of them as two races of the same species, if you like, but they are not one and the same. For instance, we know that dwarfs as described in the Eddas will turn to stone if exposed to sunlight (see *the Alvíssmál – Poetic Eddas*), they are described as black-skinned humans living in the earth or under the earth. The earth spirits which also take the appearance of dwarfs, however, are immune from harm from the sun, and even though they do live inside the earth, they also function on its surface. All characteristics here are a match: they are slower than other spirit types, they are far more solid and excellent at shaping or forming – and hence crafting. Wealth, physical power, strength, solidity and manifestation all fall within their dominion and most of the time, they manifest in the shape of males.

Rock – These spirits are very similar to the earth ones but are even more solid and dense. They actually represent the most physical of the entire spectrum of physicality and are hence the slowest, heaviest and most durable out of the two. Rocks encompass the entire scope, ranging from diamonds to pebbles found at the beach. The main difference is their scope of action: earth spirits have broader action across all things, where the earth elemental powers (or gravitational force in scientific terms) have scope. Do note, the Fjallvættir who are mountain spirits belong to this type of spirit.

Tree – where to start with this one? Tree spirits are vast ominous beings; they span huge energy systems, can be extremely territorial and absolutely hate mankind with a passion bordering on frenzy. The only ones who can safely approach a tree spirit are those with tendencies towards unity with them in their genetics and ancestral lines as did the druids of old. There is no need to explain anything more on this topic, in order to avoid tempting anyone to go looking for them and get into trouble, the only thing to note is that these spirits are the elves of nature, so many accounts exist about them, for these are the forms they adopt when projecting. One fascinating thing to note is that tree spirits multiply or congregate they merge into a single uniform forest spirit (know as the Skogvættir).

Other Plants – Everything alive has spirit of one sort or another, and this runs true for plants. Each will have a specific spirit with a scope of action defined by the plant itself. We will look at how to take advantage of thing in great detail when looking at the Seiðr of Vanaheim.

Nature – It would be impossible to follow through this description without talking about nature spirit types themselves. Their numbers are vast and most of them hate mankind. This is a long ancient hatred flowing over the course of entire generations. This makes such spirits very hard to work with and very antagonistic in their dealing with us. There is no need to explain why – anyone with any level of understanding of the world will realise this for themselves. If you are going to approach these spirits, it is important to have patience; their existence is very long in terms of time as is their viewpoint. They do not see a human being as 'a' human but rather as part of the collective of mankind. Why? Because that is what they themselves are: each nature spirit is part of the collective which is nature himself. Oh and yes, nature is masculine, not feminine. The best way to approach the entire path is that of the druid and by following the Green Man from Celtic mythology – he represents the most accurate archetype when it comes to connecting with nature. What can these spirits offer? The list is too vast to include, but to sum it up, one can describe it as being anything and everything you can think of as belonging to the natural world is within their remit (both constructive and destructive). The underlying essence of nature has within his grasp a direct route into Vanaheim for those he favours. When working with any of them, be careful: remember they view each human in the same light as the whole of humanity. Individuality is extremely hard, if not impossible, for them to grasp. They are inherently tricky to pin down to any form of agreement or position, and their underlying characteristics express themselves in harsh judgmental and final ways. Think of the heartless judge and you will get a good idea: filled with wisdom, yet ruthless in execution, who will sacrifice something happily in order to maintain the balance on a larger scale of things. If you are male, do not expect any mercy from these spirits; strength, power, ruthlessness, wisdom and physicality are what they value in all things male. Any hint of vulnerability, softness or weakness is more often than not severely abused by them. You have been warned.

Landvættir - having looked at the nature, rock, earth and tree spirits it is worth mentioning the landvættir. These are 'land spirits', they can attach to any place in the land (typically a rock or piece of land which stands out). They are considered important to the land and bring fortune, success and luck to those they protect. They also control the fertility of the land and safety upon it. Iceland has four traditional ones: the dragon (residing at Vopnafjörður), eagle (residing at Eyjafjörður), bull (residing at Breiðafjörður) and human shaped giant (residing at Vikarsskeið).

Ice – These spirits are some of the harshest you can every work with. Like the ice, they cut deep and freeze those wounds to prevent healing. They are the mistresses of the ice-cold heart, as so many fairy tales remind us. Think of the Ice Queen and you will get a very good idea of their natures. Stasis is their domain, as is defence, by freezing things into inaction, as their nature dictates preservation rather than evolution. These spirits are often sought after because they hold the keys to the prima material of (primal matter for) creation. They typically take on female forms; actually, males are extremely rare – so much so that you might see one in thousands of years of searching for it. Hence they are best formed into female forms to match their innate characteristics. Ice spirits are in their natural element dark because they reflect no light, their dominion extends over all that is dark or darkness, even as far as the black holes themselves. And in case any of you decide to develop feeling for whatever forms you are dealing with, as far as these spirits are concerned, immediately stop dealing with them; forget about them and never come back to them. Remember the tales of the ice queens in fairy tales. These spirits inspired those and not without good reason.

Rime – Rime spirits are easier to work with than either the ice or the venom ones. Their characteristics can be thought of as a mix of both the ice and venom ones and hence are a 'softening' of their harsh natures. They are primarily frost spirits but ones which focus on enabling the preservation of life rather than leading to stasis. Hence when life is frozen to be reactivated later on, these spirits come into play, as they do when transporting that life potential. They represent the gentler cooling down which is not noticed until frozen, rather than the sudden overwhelming cold of the Ice.

Snow – When ice melts and refreezes, under the influence of the air, snow is formed. Its hexagonal crystals are wonderful to observe under microscopes and when snowflakes are formed, they can take shapes of platelets, needles, columns and rime. This quick definition of snow was necessary to gain a little insight into the nature of snow spirits. They share characteristics of the air, icy cold frost, rime and water spirits. In addition to this, they hold the nature of seeding in their essence. They are the original patterns sent out to seed life, but just as importantly, they are also the new patterns imposing themselves via change on existing life. Thus the nature of these spirits is one of utmost gentleness and subtlety, involving the seeding and transformation of life, but also the harsh natures of frost and venom (via rime). Typically, they take on female forms, and as such, embodying them into a female form will yield best results.

Mist & Fog – These two are really interchangeable although traditionally, they were always referred to as mist spirits. From a scientific point of view, the difference is one of density of water in the mist which leads to fog. From a spirit point of view, mist was more efficient in carrying the characteristics of the original rime than fog. There are many different manifestations of these types of spirits, but almost all act as carriers or embodiments of one sort or another. Hence you have freezing fog, or frozen fog, ice fog, ground fog, radiation fog, steam fog and so forth. These spirits share the characteristics of water and frost – however, their primary role is obscuring and expanding the shadows. They are diffusing beings: in other words, they expand at the same rate in a given direction. Energetically, they do the same: they distort and diffuse energies.

Metal – These are very intense spirits to work with. Metal spirits are of an elemental type with intense gravitational pull; they are inflexible and have fixed ways of doing things. Due to their energy, they are extremely pure in essence but very slow to move. They are very easy to get in touch with but rather tricky to work with since you will have to do most – if not all – the work. These spirits are found in the core of the planet or in deep earth regions just like the metals themselves. Even though we do not often speak of the other planets in this particular scenario, it is important to do so. The traditional associations of specific planetary forces to metals are important here. They can be used as a guidance to determine the underlying characteristics or tint you get when working with a particular metal spirit. These spirits are excellent when it comes to stabilising things, no matter what they are. For instance, people who are constantly fidgeting and unable to sit still or relax would be excellent matches with such spirits. They also have a far greater ability to manifest than any other type due to their naturally solidifying qualities. When it comes to protection, reflection and shielding, there are the kings and queens in this domain and this is one of the most common uses of metal spirits.

Shadow – shadow or shade spirits are relatively well feared, yet not really known. Shadows first born out of Niflheim as the light and heat from Muspelheim illuminated the Ginnungagap and then the dark world itself. The first primordial shadows were cast and with them, the in-between states were born, from which the first shadowy spirits formed. These spirits are dangerous, cruel and cold as the ice world from which they were born. They are just as dark but rather than frozen darkness, they are flowing darkness. Because of their nature, they hunger for reality, and they can only exist as a result of something else or someone else's existence. These spirits can influence substance as they are the original coalescing force which split from Niflheim. They are masters of substance which holds or separates; they are the states in between matter and spirit. Many work with them, but one needs to be careful when doing so, for the shadow takes on characteristics of its host(s) and twists them into their cruel, ruthless and cold counterparts. They seek embodiment at all costs, so readily answer to any who calls upon them, but be warned: the price for such a call can most often be expensive!

Darkness – Just as with light, all forms of darkness can be worked with as if they are spirits. Here, you are connecting with a fraction of the vast essence of darkness. Just as when working with light, your assumptions need to be left behind. With darkness, it is hard for us to do because most – if not all – of our lives, we are conditioned to view it as something to be feared or something bad (or in the case of some individuals, quite in the opposite way). If you suffer from such assumptions, you run the risk of being manipulated by the spirit you intend to work with. In those cases, it is best to leave this spirit type alone and work with another. Generally speaking, the function of these types of spirits is to empower (they have an incredible amount of energy). They also have the ability to heal and harm but additionally, they have the ability to gestate new variations of things into existence. Naturally, the ability to obscure, bring one's fears to life and drown one in illusions is very much prominent with them. Like their earth, rock and metal counterparts, they too have the ability to manifest, although in a more fluid or temporal fashion. These spirits in particular have the effect of driving emotions, passions, desires to the extreme, so be extremely careful when dealing with them. Losing one's balance is very easy with them in your presence and what is worse is that you will not even notice it, unless you are very vigilant and introspective.

Venom/Poison – These spirits originate from primal powers from the yeasty venom which originated life (Ymir) from Niflheim. They are highly toxic to life in their primal forms. Why? You might wonder, for they were the sources of life. The answer is simple: yes, they were the initial components of life, but for that to turn into life, it had to go through multiple transmutations, including the melting by heat of Muspelheim, the formation into

Ymir, the growth into his hair, leading into the tree form and then the shaping by the three creator gods, before they formed man and woman. Without those transmutations and growth phases, that same yeasty venom destroys. That is what these spirits embody. They take on many forms and with much difficulty, they can embody an actual humanoid type of form. They are not really suited to it. Calling and working with them involves special runic Galdr which we will not cover at this point in time. What do they do? They poison, they cause decay and they cause bacterial growth – which is harmful as it causes unwanted transformations and so forth. Best avoided.

Creation of Spirit(s)?

As with the previous section, here come into play a few key terms which need to be understood in order to be able to maximise the practical side of things. First and foremost is the Óðr, which can be thought of as spirit within the human being. This term is quite a good fit – albeit not a perfect one – to the actual meaning of Óðr. If you prefer to, you can think of Spirit as a good term for Óðr, but do keep in mind our modern-day understanding of what spirit actually represents is very limited.

Let us look a little more in depth at what its actual meaning refers to. The most precise definition of Óðr is an outpouring (or outreaching) of the core of the Self basically, the outwards radiation of the emanations of the Spark of Self. Apologies for the high level of abstraction here, but unfortunately it is simply not possible to convey the actual meaning in layman's terminology. This reaching out is manifested via means of perception – and hence the senses, as the main perceptual tools available to mankind at this point in time. The expansion of this reaching out of the Self via perceptual mechanisms allows our Self (Spark) to grow and this in turn is the foundation of awareness, as the new perceptions are processed via the Hugr and subsequently recorded in the Minni. The functions of the Hugr then give rise to consciousness, which results in conscious awareness and intellectual capabilities arising out of the entire process.

So can we 'create new spirits'? The simple answer is no. Unless you can replicate all the perceptual abilities, create awareness, and the ability to self-reflect which all lie at the core of the outpouring of a Spark of Self you cannot create a spirit. Additionally, such creation would need to be unique for it to be universally viable. What you can create is a form with partial consciousness (a part of your own). This would be at best a temporary externalisation of you into a separate form with limited capacity and scope of action. Such beings are often termed egregores or elementals by the new age practitioners.

Final Notes for Spirit Selection

The human tendency is to always go for the 'biggest' and 'most powerful'. You should at all costs avoid this. There are a number of reasons as to why, but the most important from the outset are twofold: one, you might stumble on a spirit which highly outranks your abilities to deal with it. This opens you up to all sorts of problems and trickery, as well as energies which your Self cannot deal with properly and will have an inherently disruptive effect, whether you or the spirit want them to or not. The other important reason is that the higher or 'greater' the spirit's scope (or if you prefer, in modern terms: rank), the harder it is to interact with. You will end up being one mind calling upon a spirit which is listening to millions upon millions of such calls by minds of all sorts of magnitude. You might get a response once or twice, but there is no way to make a strong constant connection to such a spirit. It is much easier to go for a slightly less 'oh-so-high-and-mighty' spirit and make a stronger bond with them. Such bonds are also by far more beneficial as those spirits take a personal interest in those whom they work with.

As briefly touched upon, do not do this with your Fylgja. That is a very different type of spirit and an extremely personal one which needs to be integrated with the rest of your Self, not exteriorised and separated. We will be covering the Fylgja and kin-Fylgja in great detail at a later point in time.

This should suffice as a starting point. In this book, the intent is to provide a broad view of the practice with detailed information on the general practices. In the future, we will deal with more specialised spirit types as parts of more advanced studies. Just keep in mind that even if not all spirit types are discussed (that would be impossible as they are too vast in number), you can apply all the practices to whatever spirit you select to work with. Just be cautious when working with any spirit, especially the more aggressive and destructive ones (which are best avoided).

PART III – CONNECTING WITH THE SPIRIT

Approaching the Spirit

Having determined the type of spirit you want to work with, the next step involves actually finding it. This is where things get tricky and how you could go about doing this depends entirely on what skills you have developed.

In practically all the methods described below, where you are initiating the contact with your target spirit yourself, you should start by using the rune ᚠ Óss (Ansuz). Simply still your mind, chant the rune and feel the sense of ease and lightness overcome you as its indigo-blue energy pulsates within and without you. You should spend a few minutes in its energy, breathing it in, relaxing, then breathing it out. The longer you do so, the deeper and more still your mind will become. When ready, allow your intent to connect with the spirit you are after. Let its energy echo outwards beyond your mental ability to perceive and flood all that space.

Do not dissolve the ᚠ Óss (Ansuz) energy at this point. Instead, follow through with whatever method you are pursuing to its completion. Only when you are done should you will all the ᚨ Óss (Ansuz) energy to dissipate.

This puts you in a communicative trance state (a relatively mild one) where the mind remains alert but excluded from the distractions of your immediate surroundings. When your intent is made to echo outwards, the runic energy will carry it out to whatever spirit type you intended to make a connection with. It is always an excellent preliminary to do when involved with spirits. Sometimes, our minds need a bit of a sweep from our daily lives' nonsense, which obscures things. This achieves exactly that.

Spirit (Óðr) Projection

This is the most adventurous and fun method. You project in the Óðr (see *The Spirit of Húnir Awakens, Part 2*) and whilst separated from the rest of your Self, reshape it to match the typical shape of the type of spirit you are looking for. Then intend yourself to join those who are of your new type of form. It is the 'like attracts like' principle in its fullest expression.

The other variation on this practice is to abstract it one level further, which makes it easier to reach your goal but more difficult to execute. The steps involved are very similar to those given above. Here, again you project in the Óðr and separate from the rest of your Self. Instead of shaping into a form like that of the spirit you are seeking out, you fill your Óðr (whilst it is out) with energy matching the type of spirit you are seeking out. Simply filling the Óðr with that energy type will automatically reshape it. A form representing the energy type will be the end result. The advantage with this variation is that the form will be far more specific than one which you could have perceived and replicated, if you did so yourself. This way, your form will reflect your level of spiritual development in that context. To make this easier to understand, let us look at an example. Say, for instance, you are seeking to connect with a fire spirit. You separate your Óðr from the physical, fill it with fire and will it to automatically reshape in the form of a fire spirit. You would then, depending on your development, be a massive spark, a flame or a salamander form. The radiation and power flowing from you would also match your personal power level and so forth.

Either variation will work; the first requires knowledge of the form for the spirit type, while the latter requires access to the energy of the spirit type. Picking which to use will depend on whether you can perceive and replicate the form or have access to the energy type. If both are valid options for you, the latter one produces superior results as it also individualises the form you are producing, rather than having a carbon copy of the forms you might have previously perceived. It is somewhat more difficult to ground yourself in the new form, unless you are used to doing so, rather than building the form first by reshaping your Óðr yourself, it does provide much more versatility.

The important part to keep in mind is that once you have reshaped your Óðr, you need to make sure it radiated with the same energy type as that of the spirit you are seeking out – or at least the same energy type it would find in its native environment (remember, like attracts like). The next step simply involves you willing (or better yet: intending) yourself to the realm or world of that spirit type. This is pretty much an automatic process, where you simply move forward through space (imagine what it feels like being in a car driving at high speed through a tunnel where you only see the lights shift by from the windows), or, for some, a type of whirlwind motion picks them and shoots them upwards, whilst others simply have their immediate environment blur and a new one sharpen into focus, others simply 'click' into the new location. Sometimes, different types of shifting can occur depending on where you are trying to get, so no need to be alarmed if something unfamiliar takes place. If you have mastered using your Fylgja, then you can use it to shift you there as well. Once this shift has occurred and you are in the new environment, if need be, practice the '*Focal Lens of Awareness*'[9] practice to complete the shift and ground in there.

    With a solid footing in your desired destination, all you need to do is clearly intend for a matching spirit to come to you. Remember to express all you actually want to achieve in this sending out of your desire(s). When set, send out the intended offer in a pulse of energy which expands outwards until you can no longer follow it throughout the location you are in. Remember, when sending out the energy, it will be the same colour, feel and texture as that in your Óðr and in the new environment (by the way, yes, those two need to match; they always do, due to the 'like attracts like' principle).

    With a bit of luck, a potential spirit will make its presence known. If need be, communicate with it in more detail, and for goodness sake, be careful before you accept whatever it offers. Think clearly about the profound implications of each and every word! Words in other realities have power which they do not here in the human realm. For instance, a good friend of mine did a working for love and then came moaning that it failed to work. Runic work by a rune mystic (even at learner level) always produces some sort of result, so we talked. Turns out, he met this girl whom he had a strong connection with and spontaneous feeling for, but she did not reciprocate. He was most upset to find out that his rune work had worked but because he intended to find love – which he did, rather than find someone to love and be loved – he only got exactly what he asked for. He then mistakenly assumed his Galdr had failed, when in fact, it had produced 100% spot on what he intended it to. He had fallen in love – and hence, did find love. But that did not mean she loved him! The intent was one sided as was the result. Subtle distinction, but those are the types of critical distinctions which need to be taken into account when dealing with energetic realities, or you will get burnt, if not ending up in a total mess. Never ever accept to become part of the spirit's realm, or express the desire to stay there, live there, be there or whatever other twist and turn is presented, as that will bind you there permanently and eternally. Visiting is fine, because the intent is temporary. At some point, you might want to make a permanent shift but at this stage, that is definitely to be avoided. Once you have explored many facets of creation, and learnt their ups and downs, so to speak, then a more mature decision can be made on the matter.

    The other thing to be very careful about is accepting gifts from spirits in general. Remember the rules of X Gjöf (Gebo): a gift requires a gift. And this can be anything. Always be extremely specific, down to a flaw. Some take what may seem as hours of clarifications and ironing down details, when it comes to any type of exchange with a spirit. This is normal. A quick couple of sentences is not. That leaves way too many open issues, which can be exploited to no end by a skilled and intelligent spirit, always at your expense. Let us not even start with the 's/he is my friend and wouldn't do this or that'. As mentioned above, there is no such thing in spirit realms.

Having ironed out all that, you will either be shown a sign or given a name, or something which will allow you to call upon the spirit. Or, you will take some of its energy into yourself. This is an exchange which often leads to longer and deeper 'relationships' because when you exchange energy with anything, you become related to it. It works either way or both ways, but remember, you build a permanent link to that spirit. Nothing wrong with it, as long as you know what you are doing and why. It is advisable to leave this deeper form of exchange for when you have been in each other's company for a few years and had the opportunity to get to know each other. Some might jump into it, and that is fair enough – their choice. Just be aware of what you are doing. With these things, there is typically no 'undoing' what has been done.

A final word of advice on the topic of spirit exchanges and interactions at this stage. The general tendency these days is to go for the 'big bad', the most powerful of spirits you can get in touch with. This is a fundamentally flawed approach. With each spirit type, always go for the less powerful to begin with. The reason for this is simple. You are introducing or rather forcing your entire Self to deal with a new energy type which is totally alien to it, and you are opening up to it a whole new facet of reality which it did not even conceive of before. If you start this with a powerful spirit, it will overwhelm you. Do not be mistaken; it will be extremely smart and 'sneaky' about it but it will get the upper hand over you at your expense. It is absolutely imperative that you remain in control with this type of work and move at a pace where your entire Self can adapt and learn. Smaller doses of new energy help. When that energy is not the most intense available, it is easier to break down, familiarise with it, consume it, change all nine parts of the Self to be able to deal with it and so forth. Additionally, a solid working relationship is easier to build with less imposing spirits in general. They are more involved with you and happy to explore with you and show you their realms too, as well as in time, introducing you to the big players once they have gained your trust. When contacting the 'big' players in such a manner, things often progress smoother and give you more flexibility in your dealings with them. They will also value your company and are more likely to warn you against other spirits of their realm. Think of it as a 'no, don't go to him; he's a horrible one. Go see this one instead, he's way nicer' type of equivalent warning or guidance. Whereas if you do it alone with that initial call out, the first one who answers is the one who tries to get you to take them as a guide, and you have no knowledge of who it is you are dealing with. If trouble flares up, dealing with a problematic spirit of that calibre can be a total nightmare.

Quantum Jumping of Consciousness

By far the simplest method to use for those who have mastered it. All you need to do with this one is to shift into quantum consciousness within your Self. Become aware of your Óðr within your body and will the type of energy matching the spirit you are seeking out to flow into it. Because of the laws of quantum being, not only will 'like attract like' but it will also ensure that energy flows all around you. Then, funnel it into your Óðr.

Once settled, the final part you need to do is to simply send out your intent to call for the relevant type of spirit expressing your desires and what you are seeking (and offering!). You will immediately feel a presence, due to the fact that at this level, there is no space or time – everything is instant and now. From that point, proceed to ironing out the details and follow the same processes as given above.

With this method, you do not need to worry about energy exchange, names or signs to connect with the spirit in future. All you do is re-enter the quantum state and repeat this. If you feel it is easier to use a name, ask for one – or better yet, agree one with it.

Runic Trance

For those of you who have mastered runic trances, all you need to do is to use the relevant runes to induce a trance state and call out to the spirit sought. Due to the complexity of pre-requisites and trance induction (and the need for the formation of the Óðrerir within), it is impossible to include all those extensive instructions from those titles. Please refer to *The Spirit of Húnir Awakens, Parts 1 and 2,* for instructions on how to gain the required skills and ability for entering into runic trances. Certain runes are more effective than others, depending on the spirit(s) sought. Always check the High Galdr listing to ensure that the rune energy will match that of the spirits, or you will never be heard when you make your call to it. The major advantage to using this method, rather than the others, is that the spirit will be able to see you in trance here in Midgard and when it answers your call, it does so by entering your space right in Midgard.

When using the runic trance in order to connect with various spirit types, it is important to initiate the trance using the ᛉ Ýr (Elhaz) rune. Channelling the rune of divinity will enable you to gain access to the higher consciousness needed in this venture. Once that is done, all you need to do is select a rune which is suitably similar in energy terms to those of the spirit you seek. For instance, water, river and sea spirits are linked to the ᛚ Lögur (Laguz) rune, fire ones are ᚠ Fé (Fehu), flame spirits are ᚲ Kaun (Kenaz) and so forth. If in doubt, refer to High Galdr teachings for runic information.

Harmonic Meditation

This is a rather advanced method used by those who have full Seiðr skills and knowledge of Galdr. It involves shifting your own essence at the Spark of Self level to match the type of spirit you are seeking out. There is no need to go into too much detail here, with respect to this method, other than point out to those with the natural aptitude for this kind of work that they need to focus on the spirit sought and harmonise with its essence and assume an identical one. The method itself is very simple to describe, and the core of the method has been covered in *The Breath of Oðin Awakens*[10]: when in the core of yourself, simply anchor yourself there by focussing at that point for a few minutes. Then, chant the ᚹ Vin (Wunjo) rune, allowing it to fill the space with a airy-chilling dark blue energy. Intend it to harmonise you with the spirit you are seeking. Feel the same-ness build up, until you eventually feel like one of those spirit types. This sensation is the signal you are waiting for. When the feeling is present, call out for an appropriate spirit of this type to communicate with you and wait.

It should respond by a direct thought-to-mind method. Simply remain mentally still and wait for thoughts which feel as if they are coming from an external source (from outside of yourself). You reply by thinking whatever response you want to send and pushing it outwards. That is how direct mind-to-mind communication takes place.

Rather than pulling the spirit towards you, this will push you directly into its presence, from where you can proceed as with the other methods. The difference being that when a spirit is confronted by a rune mystic capable of this type of feat, an immediate form of respect and acknowledgment is experienced. When in front of the spirit, you should see its form and be able to get a name from it. When you are done, simply pull yourself back into the core of yourself and will the runic energy to dissolve until you no longer feel like the spirit. Refocus on your physical body, feel it and ground yourself in it before you return to your usual activities. Remember to make a note of the spirit name and, if you desire to, a description of its form. With these two essential pieces of information, you can proceed with the other practices.

Getting Someone Else to Do It for You

Well this one is naturally the easiest path to pursue. It is probably the most feasible for those who are embarking on this type of work for the first time ever, or those who still lack the required skill set to use one of the other methods outlined. At times, even the very skilled opt for the assistance of another when looking for spirits whose type they have trouble getting in touch with, or just do not have access to. Never discount the potential another can offer (this is, after all, one of the key lessons of the rune ᚹ Vin (Wunjo) and its energy's harmonious co-operation).

One thing to keep in mind is that you really want to avoid anyone who is working on large volumes. Such so-called 'sellers' are found online and when you look closely at their descriptions, you will immediately see that they simply do not have a clue what they are talking about. It is always best to seek out someone with whom you can build a personal connection (as how well they know you will affect how effectively they can assist you) and someone who has done this sort of thing traditionally. In other words, ideally, a Seiðr woman who has learnt the art from her mother, who has learnt it from her mother, and so forth (a Seiðr man would work just as well, although they are incredibly hard to find). It is also worth investigating what types of spirits they work with, as no one can work with any or all types, and the relationships and familiarity needed are built over a number of years, not a few attempts.

Do to keep in mind when having someone else do this for you is that most will use what are called bindings. Those literally connect the spirit to a given item. We will look at those later on, but for now, suffice it to keep in mind that you might have to rework those bindings to suit your purposes. We will look at how the runes can be used to reset the course of unsuitable bindings. When starting out, it is worth keeping to those provided because they will typically be highly restrictive to the scope of action the spirit can have. This will keep you safer than the open-ended ones we typically use. This text is aimed at skilled rune mystics who are learning a new art but already have experience and skills as their foundations, as well as an understanding of the way energy realities function. This will enable them to get out of problem situations which those without such skills would be stuck with.

Using the Name of the Spirit

In cases where you have a name for the spirit you want to work with, things are much simpler when it comes to making initial contact. Simply convert the name to runes (see Appendix A), then using High Galdr vocalise the name, allowing the energy to accumulate in your room. Once done, simply wait in passive meditation (or maintaining a silent mind state) for the spirit to make itself known to you.

Letting the Spirit Approach You

This is the simplest way of doing things. It is also the one which requires the most patience. What you need to do is go into a space where you are surrounded by the energy type matching the spirit you are seeking out. Let us say you are looking to work for a river spirit type. Go out find a nice spot by a river and sit there. Spend time meditating on what it is you are after and why. Feel the river, feel the life flowing within it, let your mind bathe in its green flowing energies (water energy is green – shades vary, but the underlying power is green, or sometimes bluish green. Rivers have a wonderful scintillating green as their water dances upon itself in flowing motion). Wait passively until the spirit approaches you. If no response comes, accept that now is not the time and come back later. Eventually, you should get a response. Persistence and patience are the keys. You can use similar techniques for other spirit types (with some exceptions, where it is impractical, due to putting you or others in danger. Safety first, spirit walking second, always).

Notes for Men

If you are male (biologically), always stick with male spirits for this work. If you opt to work with female spirits at this level, all you will achieve is an obsession with those spirits and a loss of energy (as their energy will drain yours with each and every interaction, regardless of intent. That is the nature of female energy). There are no exceptions to this rule. For those who argue that spirits are genderless because spirit is spirit and it is beyond the scope of gender, presenting that argument goes simply to show the level of lack of knowledge and experience in this field of practice. Gender and polarity exist on all levels, except the highest parts of the archetypal and in the Ginnungagap. Everything else is polarised as soon as it manifests, including Spirit itself. For this reason, Seiðr-men who work at advanced levels avoid female spirit types. These female spirits end up drawn even more to them making things rather interesting.

PART IV – BUILDING THE RELATIONSHIP

SHAPING THE SPIRIT

This is a highly controversial topic to most modern practitioners because when they go looking for spirits, they go looking for those which look like x, y or z. In other words, they are looking for something in a specific shape rather than a spirit per se. It just happens that spirits take on whatever shapes are being sought after.

For the Seiðr practitioner, this immature response will just not do. The spirit is sought out because of what it offers us in terms of capabilities, rather than because of what it looks like, which we know is only temporary, since Spirit itself is actually formless and spirits manifest in forms which match with their characteristics and functions, according to the universal laws of attraction. It will take on a form which represents symbolically its capabilities and characteristics. This means if it is female by nature, it will not be able to adopt a proper male form, and if it tries to, it will typically be a type of she-male where there is an overly feminine quality to the masculine and throws it completely off balance. In other words, it cannot adopt fragmented energy types which do not correspond to its nature. Trying to force a spirit into a form which does not match its inherent nature will cause friction in between you and it, to the point where it will be forced back to its own realm. It is of vital importance when working with any type of spirit to ensure that whatever impulses are received, they are not from yourself but come from the spirit. It takes a little practice to distinguish the two, but those of you who have worked through the other books will have (hopefully!) gained sufficient skill in order to be aware of the difference between information coming from within or an external source.

What most Seiðr practitioners will do is to either perceive a direct form of the spirit in its natural state or select a form which they build that matches the spirit's nature and characteristics. The closer and truer the match, the better that spirit will be able to express its nature and vice versa.

Once the form is selected, the next step involves building it up in one's mind. You must be able to visualise it perfectly. Remember the teachings from *The Spirit of Húnir Awakens* when it comes to visualisation! Include all the senses and other tricks outlined therein. Having established shape, half the work is done!

Imposition of Form and Naming

With shape comes form and name. For form to be established, you infuse spirit into shape and this then becomes the basis for building its Hamr. The shaping you have done and the visualisation of that shape gives it the blueprint foundation it needs to actually build an fully functional Hamr. The other thing it will need is a name.

Depending on how you have contacted it, you might already be aware of its name, or if someone else did it for you, they might have given you a name to use. In any case, communicate with the spirit and ensure they are happy for you to use that given name. Some can be very secretive about their names and the possibility can arise that they will want you instead to name them or have another name used as a matter of course. This avoids their actual names from being spoken at the wrong time and in the wrong place. When it comes to you actually naming them, it also creates an additional strengthening of the bond in between you. It's not an absolute must by any stretch of the imagination but it can be a helpful boost when starting out.

Having gained shape and name, it is time for you to move onto the actual forming of the spirit. This will result in a stable form it can use to manifest, the foundations of the blueprints for its Hamr and a damn good solid connection to yourself.

Start by using the preparatory steps outlined above. Then when you feel the presence of the spirit behind you, you will visualise the shape you have been working on as standing next to it. For instance, if the spirit is standing behind your right shoulder, visualise the shape as being behind the left shoulder or vice versa. What you do next is intend the spirit to infuse the shape. Simply sending out an actual intent will act as a magnet and pull one towards the other, until the spirit is absorbed into the shape. In cases where that fails, visualise the energy of the spirit flow into the shape, intensifying the flow until it is all bound within that shape. Either way, you should now see the fully established form of the spirit with its energy contained within that form and glowing out through the outer edges in the same way as an aura would. The only difference this outer glow will be only an inch or two at most. If it is any more than that, you need to spend a little time meditating that the form contains the spirit and its energy – otherwise, it will just spill out completely.

Assuming all has gone right (if not, keep on with the practice until it does), now name the spirit inside the form. You are, in effect, now naming it as a whole complete being rather than just the spirit. This is where you would use the secondary name if it has asked you to, or the one you intend to name it with. If using the actual spirit's name, then use it instead. This naming locks the spirit and form together, or to be more accurate, fuses them. From that moment on, whenever it appears to you or manifests in your reality (Midgard), it will use that form. Unless it has to act as pure spirit – then it simply projects out of it as you would do out of your Lik.

Understanding the Spirit Type and Helping it Shape Itself

Certain spirits have certain characteristics in terms of shape. For instance, all elves are thinner in frame and have the traditional pointed ears everyone here is familiar with. Most of them are rather delicate, even those who are extremely masculine; there is a subtle flow to it which humans are not capable of. Here in Midgard, masculinity is associated with bulk strength and hence mass, whereas for elves, this is not the case. They can maintain the flow, with rapid sharp movements which they are notorious for. Dwarfs are dark skinned, love dark spaces, the earth and subterranean places, hate the sun and light (it is actually deadly for some of them, according to the Eddas – see *Alvíssmál*). Sexual spirits often have extremely attractive bodies, are highly symmetrical – one could almost say perfect looking, which expresses the feminine or the masculine in what we perceive the most perfect of ways. Dark spirits are darkness embodied: cold and harsh. You can easily use the Eddas and other Sagas to get descriptions of various spirits according to traditional sources. Icelandic accounts are also available to compliment your research.

Other spirits are known to other traditions, such as elemental ones – in Norse texts, the dwarfs figure very prominently as earth-based spirits. There are, however, fire spirits, air spirits, water spirits, frost spirits, mist spirits and so forth.

Regardless of spirit type, each one will have certain base characteristics which need to be defined in their shapes and forms. Learning about those will help you build a more effective and appropriate form for it.

The other way a good shape can be used as a basis, assuming that your senses are developed, is to look at the spirit itself. By doing so whilst going into trance, you will be able to read its energies and get a flow of symbolic representations for it. Doing it in this way will give you an extremely useful and accurate set of characteristics to build into the ultimate form for the spirit to wield.

Building an Energy Body (Hamr) for the Spirit

It is time to take the final step in formation for the spirit. What you are going to be doing is concentrating the spirit's energy into the form you have been working on. This has a number of effects which you are after. First and foremost, it will gradually make it more solid. By 'more solid', what is meant is that after sufficient concentration of energy into a given form takes place for a spirit, it starts to gain a type of matter, and this in turn makes it more than just energy but less than matter. It places that spirit on the borderline in between the two, where from time to time, it can step from one into the other and vice versa. This is ultimately what all these spirits seek but can never achieve on their own. The other thing is that it will help ensure that the energy of the spirit is indeed contained in the form rather than spilling out of it, as if it was a leaking waterbed. Thirdly, it will help you perceive it more accurately and more intensely. Additionally, since it now has an artificial type of Hamr, it will be able to affect the energy side of reality in addition to the mental side of reality.

The practice is actually quite simple, providing you have undertaken the above mentioned forming and naming work. You need to start with the preparatory steps given above, but by now, you will no longer feel just the spirit standing behind you but the form it has. Mentally repeat its name (the one you assigned during formation) until its presence solidifies behind you. Then, visualise the vast space around you changing from being empty to being filled with the energy type matching that of the spirit you are working with. It might take a little time to split your focus on maintaining sensation and perception of the spirit, along with maintaining the focus on the energy around you. Practice makes perfect!

You will notice that the spirit's presence becomes more intense, as if there is more 'life' to it. That is natural. It is, after all, now bathing in an environment filled with its native energy type. What you need to do next is pull in as much of this energy into its form as you can. Do so a few times only to begin with, and then each time you do, expand your pull phases by one. End the practice and allow all the leftover energy to fade away, until you are once more left in an empty endless space with the formed spirit behind you!

Building and Enhancing the Connection

Once you have established who the spirit you are going to work with is and its basic characteristics and it has acknowledged youand its form is solidifying, you are then ready to move onto the next step, which is to strengthen your connection with it.

Let us be clear from the get go with this: work and regular practice are needed here. This is the one time where the more you do, the better result you get. It does not really matter what the quality of your interaction is. What matters is how often you interact. This is essential and fundamental. For the scientifically minded, think of it in terms of neural networks: the more often you trigger the same connections, the stronger they become. The fitness focussed will understand this well: the more often a movement is done, the easier and more reflexive it becomes and so forth. Keep your interactions regular and consistent. It matters little whether one interaction is of great quality and value and the other 10 are poor or barely noticeable. What matters is that you do them often.

Naturally, we all want as good an interaction as possible, so here are a few practices which will improve the quality of your interactions with the spirit. But do keep in mind what has been said above. Keep it regular; there is no need to do long complex 30-minute meditations each time. Those can be far and few in between.

With each of these, the initial steps are the same. You will start by sitting in a comfortable position (no arms or legs crossing, as that inhibits energy flow). Close your eyes and relax. Allow the world to fade from your mind, forget the daily hustle and bustle. If you are skilled in trance work, go into trance. If not, simply keep relaxing and let yourself switch off without losing focus.

Then visualise yourself in an infinite expansive empty space. Having established that setting, if you have an object linking the spirit to you, hold onto it and focus on it. Otherwise, just focus on the spirit as you saw or experienced it when seeking it out. Spend a few moments thinking about it, then intend the spirit to be right next to you. Spirits most often manifest behind us, often giving the impression that someone is looking at us and making us turn around from time to time, or as is often the case for women, it can make them uneasy and stressed. Men have a tendency of completely dismissing the impression and short-circuiting the entire process. DO NOT do that! Just acknowledge it and keep focussing on it. This will amplify it and bring it even more into the remit of your conscious perceptions. At this point, you are ready to start. Incidentally, just doing this will strengthen your connection in and of itself!

Energy Bathing

This first permutation involves you and the spirit bathing in each other's energy. The way it is done is quite simple. Expand your auric field and with it, wrap around the spirit until it is contained within. Then pull it slightly inwards. This might sound tricky but once practiced, you will find it easy to do. You are using the energy of your aura to pull it into the aura, just as you would use your hand to grab hold of something and pull it towards you. As you do so, intend the spirit to be contained in your auric field.

After a few moments, ask it to expand its own energy field WITHIN yours. This will feel peculiar the first few times you do it because it is in effect an alien energy spreading throughout your own. Depending on the spirit you are working with, different sensations and perceptions will surface and flood you. Just acknowledge them but do not get distracted by them.

The next step simply involves meditating on how you are both sharing something of yourselves with each other.

Energy Exchange

With this version, the energy interaction gets much deeper, but also do take note that here, you are actually exchanging, rather than just experiencing each other's energies. This will create a permanent bond. In energetic terms, it also makes you related to each other very much as genetics make us physically related to our siblings and ancestors here. Most will disregard the importance of this warning. Keep in mind that whatever happens, this bond is never truly removed until the death of your Hamr and in some cases, not even then. Make sure you take this into account before you undertake this sort of exchange, especially when it intensifies.

The actual practice is simple, either be as close to naked as possible or actually naked. Some do this in the shower every morning, which if you have time to spare and are not running out of the house like a madman to make it into work on time, is a good way of practicing this. If not, then lying down on the bed or sitting comfortably is another. Whatever you do, do not do this whilst in a bath. Slipping into deeper trance state is practically a given, and being in a bath full of water in trance is an extremely dangerous thing to do. There is no need to rush and take stupid risks.

Having run through the preparatory steps outlined above, intend the spirit to touch you. Feel its hands on your body, but do not attempt to direct them, let it do so. All you need to focus on is the act of feeling whatever sensations are picked up. Here, you have the advantage that your body will help by sensing directly – assuming you have worked through *The Blood of Lóðurr Awakens*, you should have no problem at this stage. A blending of biological sensing with energetic sensing will make things very real indeed. Being in the shower will amplify this as well, as it is not only conducive to transference but also will have your body in hyper-sensitive drive, in terms of feeling (since you are feeling the water running down all over your body anyway).

Once the feeling of being touched has surfaced and stabilised (you have felt it more than a few times and are aware of it), intend the spirit to pour its energy into you when it touches you. This will amplify everything. You will perceive it and its tactile intrusions even more. You can, at this point, direct it to shift its touching wherever you want. But do be wary of getting sexual at this early stage; the flaring up of sexual sensations will overload your focus and you will lose 'sight' of the spirit's touch.

Only after this is very familiar territory should you move in that direction.

A Physical Anchor?

Traditionally, spirits, as well as self-created energetic beings, were given an object to anchor themselves into physically. This is the root of so many blessed statues, cursed objects and haunted places. However, whether you opt for this or not will depend on how you intend to interact with the spirit. If you decide to use methods which pull you out of the physical (in other words, you work from the lower up into the higher levels of frequency or lower density), you will want to avoid this. However, if you want to make the spirit as effective physically as possible and you are working from above to below, you will want to have something the spirit can anchor into. All that you need to do is to pull the energy which matches the spirit type and fill an object, space, statue, with it intending it to be a permanent home for that spirit whilst it is on Earth in your realm. What you use is always a matter of personal preference and seldom matters further than that. As long as the energy you fill it with matches ('like attract like' laws!), it will work.

Some will be tempted to use their own body to serve as an anchor for the spirits they work with. You should avoid doing so at all costs. Our physical bodies are not capable of sustaining such energy charges for long. Not only will the charge dissipate or be processed as part of your energy system, but it will also disrupt your natural energy flow, causing all sorts of issues, both energetic and potentially health-wise too. It is not wise to over-expose yourself to one energy.

PART V – ENHANCING SPIRIT SYMBIOSIS

Communicating With Spirits

A few quick notes are necessary when it comes to communication. It is vitally important to always keep in mind that when spirits use language to communicate with us, they are direct. What is meant is the words used are all that is meant. More often than not (with the exception of some few spirit types), what they say is exactly and only what is meant. The same rules apply to your own communications, so select your words with EXTREME caution and care. There is no such thing as 'I said this but meant that' or 'I didn't mean it this way or that'. Everything is done literally to the word. When entering into any sort of agreement, always think every single word over and over again, and then again and again. Look for all the negative side effects of whatever you are agreeing to. You have to be extremely cautious when dealing with them, no matter how much of a 'friend' you think they are. Remember, each spirit is a fragment of massive impersonal forces in creation. Friendship is a human concept only! Never let a spirit tempt you into anything you are uncertain about. Especially when it comes to visiting their realms. Countless types of them will go to extraordinary lengths to try and trap you there and once trapped, it is practically always forever.

Always remember, you are ultimately held responsible and suffer the consequences of all you ask of the spirit(s). Yes, even knowledge can be a very costly thing to seek out. A proper Seiðr practitioner will have to provide their spirits with the energy and matter for them to act – anything less than that will make you a tool of the spirit, even though you might think you are in control. Always fully charge your Hamingja and only use as much Megin as you can afford to spare (see *The Breath of Oðin Awakens*).

Step 1 – First approach

You will have to work in a number of different ways, depending on how you have set things up. They all eventually end up being the same, with the exception of a few initial steps to deal with those differences.

If you have an object which serves as a link to the spirit – this could be an item it is connected to (otherwise labelled as 'bound to'), a runic spirit anchoring infuser (as its name implies, these devices anchor the spirit into our reality), or a place it has a connection with – you will have to get hold of that item and keep it in contact with your body for at least a few hours a day. Should the anchor be a place, simply go and sit as close to its centre as possible. This will allow the energy of the spirit and your own to intermix. Depending on the spirit type you are working with, this might be more or less of a challenge. So take it slow. If it becomes overbearing, then stop, remove yourself from it and try again later. Eventually, you will adapt to the (typically) higher-energy types.

In cases where there is no object or place linked with the spirit and you have opted not to create one, simply skip this step.

Step 2 – Connecting

After Step 1 has produced a type of comfortable presence with the new energy (the spirit's energy), you may proceed. For Step 2, you will sit in meditation, clearing your mind of everything from the outside and focusing within. Once your thoughts have calmed down a little, you are ready. For those of you who have mastered clearing the mind (see 'Mind Scattering - Internal Dialog' p.11 - *The Spirit of Húnir Awakens - Part 2*), use those practices.

In your mind, repeat the name of the spirit over and over again. Allow your sense of feeling to open up and reach out. Doing so is easy; simply try to feel whatever is around you. Because you have just silenced your mind, you should experience yourself in what appears to be empty space with just you there. That is what turning inwards does to our minds; we reconnect to the Hamr where there is just us and nothing else. Although that is not strictly the case, it is how our minds perceive that state of being. We will look at this phenomenon at a later point in time when dealing with the Hamr. Keep on repeating its name and keep your senses open to whatever comes through. In cases where you need to, feel free to refocus your mind on the object/place you are using to connect with the spirit while calling out its name mentally. Eventually, an image of its form will pop into your mind and a clear sensation of it will be felt. This can take more or less time, depending on how well your perceptions are developed. Persistence is the key!

A few things you can look for: when the initial approach happens, providing your body is kept still, you will notice a pressure on the upper part of your nose. As if the air has a slight area of tension to push through at the top of nose (inside the nasal passage, just about one quarter or half of an inch before it reaches the bridge, in between the eyes). Relax and let things flow. This results in an opening of the channels and a sensation of a totally free, almost effortless flow of air through your nasal passageways. Quite often, this will be followed by a slight pressure at the point in between the eyes. It is important to look out for this because it is always subtle and can be easily missed. In case you feel pain, something is not going right, so stop immediately, wait for three days, then repeat. Should this reoccur, stop permanently. Get checked to ensure it is not a medical issue causing the pain. Should that come back clear, try with another spirit. If it repeats, then yours is not the path of the spirit walker. Our bodies often speak to us in this fashion – if only we listened when they do, so much many problems would be avoided!

Providing all goes well, use the ᚠ Óss (Ansuz) and ᛜ Ing (Ingwaz) runes. Unleash their energy, and chant their names until the entire emptiness is filled with the dark blues with sensations of lightness (for ᚠ Óss (Ansuz)) and a sense of heavy density (for ᛜ Ing (Ingwaz)). To avoid confusion, we are using both runes in a manner that forces them to manifest in the dark blue spectrum of colour (hence light) on purpose. This is generally the primary one for spirit walking, and by forcing all the rune's energies to manifest in this manner, you are deliberately focusing them in on this purpose. We will look at other uses elsewhere.

Having the runic energy there, bathe in it and start repeating the spirit's name once more. You should notice a strongly amplified result this time round. When you are done, will the rune energy to dissolve until it is completely dissipated and you are once more in empty space.

Step 3 – Listening, Feeling and Seeing

This is the tricky step; you will begin by completing Step 2 as given above. Rather than dissolving the runic energy, leave it there. Allow it to flood your ears and ask the spirit to communicate. Remember this golden rule: when working with the spirit in this way, you are doing so on the mental level, hence you ask it using your thoughts and you listen using the ears of your mind. When it replies, you will experience an odd thing, which can only be described as words being placed into your mind but you have the distinct knowledge and sensation that they come from somewhere else (in other words, not from your own mind, as your thoughts do). This is tricky to pick up, but practice makes perfect (as does knowledge of your own mind), and in time, you will be able to immediately pinpoint what originates in you and what is external.

With the sense of feeling things are much easier, you use your energy field (otherwise known as the aura) and reach out. A type of melding happens at the edge of it, and the spirit interacts directly in that way. It basically steps into it. Remember, your physical body is a hardened part of your Hamr, hence it can interact with that too. More often than not, this is experienced by us as an electric spark for the high-energy spirits or as a gentle caress for the softer ones.

Seeing is very similar to listening. Keep your mind blank and use the ᛞ Dagur (Dagaz) rune. Unleash its electric dark blue energy, along with a sensation of electric sparks or static. Then pull all that energy into the eyes. Remember, if the tension gets too strong, then STOP – you have as much energy as your bodies can handle. No point harming yourself. Take this seriously. You have been warned. Keep the energy in your eyes and dissolve the rest outside of them. Intend that ᛞ Dagur (Dagaz) power to increase your sight and, in particular, to allow you to see the spirit. Keep the physical eyes closed (you are working on the mental, not physical, so there is no need for physical sight). What will happen is that the image of the spirit will be projected into your mind directly. It is not the eyes that see it per se. The difference here is that the details – often very minute details – will be so sharp and distinct that they would be impossible (or extremely improbable) to have been imagined (unless you spent weeks upon weeks building it into the most minute details, in which case it would be a type of artificial thought form – this is why we work with a general form and avoid going into tiny details). When you are done, push the energy from within your eyes back out into the space around you, then dissolve it until there is no more. If this is also the end of your work for the time being, remember to dissolve the underlying ᚠ Óss (Ansuz) and ᛜ Ing (Ingwaz) runic energy as well!

As you progress in your work, the mental shifts into the energetic. It is a natural progression, just as the manifestation is. Your senses will also shift. The feelings will become almost indistinguishable from a physical sensation, apart from one key fact: they will be far more intense than any physical ones could ever be. The sight, even with closed eyes, will no longer be just an image projected into your mind's visual mechanism. Instead, when having your eyes closed and looking into the blackness ahead, you will see in it, and what you will see is the spirit. When listening, the words will be 'heard' as if they were physical.

This all takes time. Be patient and persistent. Here you are teaching all your bodies (including your shadow (Sal)) and trying to use them synchronously. They will all need different amounts of training and taming.

Step 4 – Quick Sync

When the time comes that all you want is to just connect in a quick and easy manner, then providing you have worked through the above steps, all you need to do is simply take hold of the object (if you have one) with the link to the spirit, close your eyes and repeat (mentally) the ᚹVin (Wunjo) rune, allowing its cool breezy dark blue energy to wrap around you. Then meditate on the fact that you are in harmony with the spirit. Keep your mind blank (or as silent as you can) and let the senses pick up whatever they do. For men who have trouble with this, just think of the spirit as your best buddy! Keep that in mind when trying to communicate and connect. Works wonders.

A few notes: you can do this with any spirit. For those of you who follow or work in multiple traditions, even non-Norse spirits work in exactly the same way. Even those working with Gods and Goddesses can use the same methods, although that takes an incredible amount of time and effort to produce results. The only time these methods will not work is when dealing with formless abstractions. In Norse mythology, we have the nameless Eagle, which is in fact a formless abstraction (more on that at a later time). In Christianity, the concept of 'God the Creator' or 'Holy Spirit' is another such abstraction. In the New Age movement, what is referred to as Spirit (as in The Spirit) is another. With those, completely different methods need to be used. We will review some in rune work, where runes are used to connect with pure abstractions.

Spirit Feeding

The concept of spirit feeding or gifting of foods to it appears in many cultures and takes on many differing forms. The end goal of the practice, no matter what form it is undertaken in, is to provide grounded physical energy for it to consume. In some cases, this food is not only offered to the spirits but also then consumed by human beings. This should be avoided simply because that food is then void of energetic substance and consuming it feeds the Lik but it starves the Hamr. Food which replenishes the one and starves the other is extremely dangerous spiritually and energetically speaking, since it will cause the starved part of the Self to become envious of the feeding of those parts which are fed. This creates inherent disharmony and disrupts the natural flow of the Self, resulting in a whole range of problems, due to the Hamr retaliating against the Lik.

Most who start out will dabble in spirit feeding in some form or other because it is the only method they have available to provide quasi-physical substance to the spirits they work with. In our case, this just will not do. We have such a wide array of skill sets and abilities to achieve not only the same, but also highly superior results.

What you will be doing is creating substance from energy or pulling substance from the environment and using that to feed the spirit(s) you are working with. As usual, there are a few different permutations to the available methods we have in order to achieve this:

1. Forming substance using the ᛒ Bjarkan (Berkano) and ᛟ Óðal (Othala) runes from an existing energy
2. Pulling the substance out of the physical environment
3. The third one we will not discuss here

We are only going to look at the first and second methods. The third is, let us say, what one could term as highly 'controversial' from the human perspective.

Runic Creation of Substance

This method requires an existing pool or source of energy to work from. You can use your own, or energy gathered from other practices which you can draw from. All you need to do is go into a slight trance or relaxed state and '*Spirit Shift your Óðr*' into the shape of the ᛒ Bjarkan (Berkano) rune (see *The Spirit of Húnir Awakens - Part 1*, p.37). Once complete, allow the energy you are going to use to flow through you (whilst maintaining your Óðr's shape in that of the rune). As it does, will it to concentrate. Pool more and more energy and make it flow throughout the shape of the ᛒ Bjarkan (Berkano) – which is you. Chant the rune's name or chant it using High Galdr. This will cause a massive 'hardening' of the energy as well as a decrease in volume (the amount will lessen, due to concentration). Once you are comfortable with the degree of condensation, you can then form it into any shape and offer that to the spirit, or pool it in water/food and offer that. Alternatively, a more direct method is to simply have the spirit touch you and will this substance to flow from the point of contact from you into the spirit's hands and arms. Whatever method you use to make this transference is irrelevant. Once it has completed, reshape your Óðr back to the shape of your Lik and slowly shift out of trance.

Here, you are in effect moving energy to substance at a cost of energy. It is one of the ways in which things are manifested from the purely energetic into the physical. Do remember only to do this with spirits you are working with yourself. Do not do this with random ones, with spirits asking you to, or with spirits that other people work with, even if you know those people. Doing these types of practices as a favour for a family member or friend is completely a no go. Why? Because it binds you to the spirit worked with, irrespective whether you want it to or not. If you do not want to be bound with the spirit, do not do it, simple as that.

Pulling Substance out of the Environment

This method is both simpler and more troublesome because it requires the development of specific skills to execute. It has the advantage that you can get vast amounts of substance without having to form it. You do not require the ability to shape shift the Óðr and you can make much greater amounts of substance flow to the spirit. The big disadvantage is that it channels only Midgard (Earth) environmental substance; you cannot produce custom substance from a specific energy. Why should that matter? Well, with the previous method, you can produce substance from, say, the energy type of the spirit you are working with, rather than tainting it with whatever is found in your environment. With this one, you will be flooding it with whatever substance is found in your environment and only that which you are in harmony with yourself. For instance, if you want to gain substance which is found, say, in aggressive and violent environments, you will only gain access to those if you are an aggressive person and within that type of environment (a place where aggression is encountered). However, if you are a peaceful person, you will not be able to channel that type of substance sufficiently well for this. Even if you find yourself in a situation where aggressive behaviour takes place, unless you have a predisposition towards it yourself, you will not synchronise with that underlying substance – or energy. The same runs true of the opposite polarity; we are only using aggression as an extreme example here to make it stand out.

One substance you will have access to is that of Midgard (Earth) as a general one. Additionally, you will have access to whatever you are naturally synchronised with. The method is actually very simple: first, you will need to establish a connection with pure substance, learn to manipulate it and then use it.

Simply sit down and relax in a semi-darkened room. Or if you prefer to do this outdoors, make sure there is some sort of structure about to focus on: a building or trees or even a street lamp will do. Obviously, you do not want to try this in full sunlight or strong lights; ideally, just before the night is due, when it is still light but not too light.

Start by chanting or repeating the ᛟ Óðal (Othala) rune, allowing the heavy solid dark blue energy to pervade all the space about you. If you are in a room, it will fill that room; if you are in nature or open space, allow it to form a shape with you in its centre. Working with a cube of ᛟ Óðal (Othala) energy or a rectangle works very well. For the more adventurous, other shapes are usable. The important thing is you are standing in its centre point. Focus on the corner of a wall, if indoors, or the corner of a building or the branches of a tree. Find that spot which is semi-obscured and focus on it whilst relaxing. Do not move your gaze away from the selected spot. Relax and will yourself to see the substance from which everything is formed. This might take quite a few attempts but persistence is key with this. You might notice a slight shimmering about the spot you are focusing – ignore this, as it is just an optics trick. What you want to wait for is a type of dimming in that very spot, as if it is darkening but not dark. Some might perceive it as a deepening of the focal spot. Once you have that, you focus on the immediate space all around it (but do not shift your gaze away from your original spot). You will eventually be able to notice that the space around your selected focal spot has a type of silvery-black dark cloudy substance swirling around it. For the first few times, simply practice getting to the point where you can perceive it.

Once perception of this substance has been gained, the next step when focusing on your selected spot is to will that substance to coalesce even further. Using intent, will it to gather more and more. Once you have a certain volume – or what is better termed as a viscosity of it – you can will it to flow anywhere you like. Practice getting to this point a few times. Once mastered, then practice making it flow left, right, up, down and so forth. When mastered, you can make it flow to you or to your spirit. Start by feeding this to the spirit you are working with in small doses, then increase them a little each time. Eventually, you should be able to do so with larger and larger amounts of substance or from any spot in your immediate environment you choose to focus on. You will see that the more substance and the longer you do this, the more tangible the spirit you are working with becomes.

When you are done, simply allow the ᛟ Óðal (Othala) energy to dissolve completely (but not the substance you have gathered for your spirit, or for the spirit you are working with).

Remember when you work with a spirit it is your duty to ensure it has the energy it needs. That is the unspoken agreement in between the two of you. Failing to provide it with sufficient energy will result in it feeding off your own.

Feeding the Spirit with Megin

For those of you who have worked through *The Breath of Oðin Awakens*, you can feed the spirit with your Megin. Be very careful here, as it is an extremely effective method but it comes at a price: it will weaken you (and all your bodies) if you are not careful. Remember to always recharge your Hamingja and give it at least a few days in between sessions for your reserves to rebalance.

The practice is incredibly simple. Focus in on the Hamingja and pull some of its Megin out, allowing it to flow down your right arm. Make it accumulate there. The spirit will make contact with your right hand. You will feel this; it is a very distinctive sensation, which cannot be mistaken, allow the Megin to flow from your arm straight into the spirit. When done, interrupt the flow and will it to disconnect.

Spirit Gifting

Another common occurrence within the modern-day adaptations of these practices involves giving so-called 'gifts' to spirits on the basis that they like such things and find pleasure in them. With this one, it is important to realise that this is utter sentimental 'childish' nonsense. Gifting of trinkets to spirits is nothing more than an imposition of human childhood behaviours on spirits, which are furthest from humans – let alone human children.

The only practical purpose such behaviour (gifting) could serve is to act as a focal point for you to connect with the spirit. However, since the skills and methods available at our disposal are 'light years' ahead of these types of trinket gestures, we connect with the spirits we work with in far more direct and conscious ways, rendering this type of gifting pointless. A gift can be used in terms of gods, where they serve as vessels for them to connect with us – but even in such a capacity, they are some of the most primitive ways to achieve such connections and should be avoided.

PART VI – WALKING WITH THE SPIRIT

Merging With the Spirit
Shared Experiencing

This is probably one of the most exciting and enjoyable practices to be done with a spirit. Naturally, you will need to have formed it first, providing you have gained at least some basic skill with 'Óðr Projection or Shapeshifting the Óðr', as outlined in *The Spirit of Húnir Awakens (Parts 1 and 2)*. If you can, you are ready to go.

The practice is very straightforward but does take a little time to fully unfold its potential. Before jumping into it, always make sure you have set your ground rules with the spirit you are going to be doing this with, and have arranged what will be done during your merged state and who will be in control at what points and for how long. What you do is either enter into a mild trance or a deep state of relaxation, letting go of the world at large. Then, depending on which route you prefer, do either:

1. Shift into the Óðr and reshape your Óðr to match the form of the spirit. As you do so, intend to be inside of it. Here we are making practical use of the 'like attracts

like' principles, where we match the form of the spirit in our own spirit. This in turn attracts us to what we are now like, which is the spirit's form and hence the spirit itself. Next, use the X Gjöf (Gebo) rune. Chant it from within your spirit (which should now be standing outside of your body, facing the spirit you are working with), and allow its airy dark blue energy to carry your energy into the spirit's and the spirit's into your own. They will keep on mixing in this fashion until the two of you merge into one.

The end result is that your awareness and your senses will be propelled into the spirit's form, where you will both blend into each other, occupying it simultaneously. This will be a reflex type of trigger and unless you ground in it, you will be pushed back out the very next moment. Before that happens, intend for the two of you to blend energetically (if you have done the 'Energy Bathing' practice as given in the connection section above, this will be easy to do). Doing this, you will share your thoughts with the spirit and its own will be shared with your awareness. Perceptions will flow through one another, back and forth. The important part is to submit to the energy flow and just allow it to happen. If you are a man, this might be difficult, but since it is key to the Seiðr training, you should be able to trigger this passivity at will, by now. As things settle down, you will need to communicate with the spirit as to what you will both be doing next or what is desired. Always be careful in how and what you ask or how you express your desires. All the warnings of intent and dealing with spirits apply in each and every interaction you have with them! Especially during these types of practices.

Depending on your purpose, either you or it will take what can be termed the 'driving seat' – in other words, control of the spirit and form. If you intend to visit its realms, for it to show you things and so forth, allow it to take the driving seat and remain in the background, experiencing and watching. If you are going to experience things (especially in our level of Midgard) from its perspective, you then must take the driving seat and it will be present in the background, experiencing and learning instead. Such setting is most beneficial when you are teaching a spirit how to use a human type of form, especially for spirits who have never been human before or are unfamiliar with it. As a general rule, the further the native realm of the spirit you are working with, the less familiar it will be with our forms and how we control and use them in our own reality.

2. The second method involves you projecting out of your Lik in your Oðr. Once you have separated, you spill the Oðr of yours into the form of the spirit and initiate the energy merging as outlined above. The rest of the practice is exactly the same. The main advantage to using this method is that a stronger separation takes place from your own Lik and Self. It also yields much better results when you have to take the driving seat in the spirit form as well as when teaching a spirit how to use the human form. In practically all other instances, using the first of these two methods seems to be more effective.

To end both practices, you will need to get back to your Lik – assuming, of course, you actually left its proximity in the first place. If not, then you will already be there. You once more use the rune X Gjöf (Gebo) but this time, intend its airy flowing dark blue energy to pull your energies out of the spirit you are working with more and more, until you are standing once more as a spirit facing your working partner. Simple intent is required to trigger this un-blending of the two – it does the trick and you will feel the deep unity start to lessen and lessen and lessen... until the 'I' resurfaces completely. As it does, the energies will look like interlocking threads, but not the same threads anymore. If you have projected the Óðr before merging in the spirit form, pull all of your energies out of the spirit form as if you were projecting out of your own body again, but this time, you are projecting out of the spirit form. You will find yourself standing in your own Óðr reshape it to the form of your Lik. Finally, step back into the Lik or just intend to return to it. Both should work fine, and which to use is a matter of preference. For some reason, the Minni writes the memories of the experiences down better when you actually take the time and effort to consciously step back into your Lik.

The reshaping triggers the 'like attracts like' principles and can pull you back into your Lik. Should this happen, all you do is re-establish what your own body (Lik) feels like and then become aware of its immediate environment (in other words, where you are sitting or lying down, and so forth).

The spirit will be standing somewhere close during this separation and will be establishing its own 'imprint' on the form once more. A type of self-grounding occurs for it to reassert its dominion in the spirit form without you or your presence there. When done, make sure that your energies are all within your own spirit and all of its energies are in its own form or body. You do not want any bleed-over, otherwise you risk pulling part of it back into your own body and giving it a gateway for possession at a later point in time. If you are going to enter into those kinds of practices, it is best they are done at the right time, rather than leaving unfinished bits and pieces of others practices activate in the background. Always be in control. You can always will the X Gjöf (Gebo) energy to dissolve away. This takes away the functional power responsible for mixing of both your energies and further disentangle the two of you. When done, simply re-enter your body and allow the Óðr (your spirit) to merge with the physical.

It is a good idea to have some food, or at least a good strong coffee to ground your mind back in the here and now, after this type of experience. Needless to say, this is an extremely powerful practice which can literally open up endless possibilities for you. You will be able to, in terms of human minutes and hours, gain entire years' worth of experiences and knowledge in this manner and in a direct concrete way. Additionally, because Seiðr practice often involves use of multiple spirit types, you will be able to widen and broaden your life experiences in remarkable ways, just by connecting with additional spirits! But whatever you do, remember your Lik and at all costs, avoid getting lost or bound to their realms and realities. That would pretty much be the end of your adventuring throughout creation. Always, always remember you will carry an imprint of the energy types and experiences you have in this manner, and just as you do with your daily life, those imprints will affect you on all levels of your Self.

Going to Its Native Realm(s)

This practice has been hinted at above. Here, the goal is for you to merge with the spirit you are working with and take a walk in its own realm/world. Remember to establish the rules which you are comfortable with before starting this practice. You will also need to set clear agreements as to what the spirit can and cannot do while it is in control. In this practice, you are the passenger at first. After you have acquired a lot of experience in this capacity and learnt about its home realm, you can take the driving seat. Eventually, you will also master the energy of that realm and be able to go there on your own, by infusing your own spirit with that same energy. For the time being, allow it to show you the wonders of its native home. Always remember to be specific that this is a temporary visit and that it needs to bring you back to your physical body (don't just use the term 'body', use 'physical body' and 'on Earth in your native time' when setting this criteria), otherwise spirits can be tricky and will try to trap you there.

This movement is achieved using either of the previously given two practices of merging with the spirit in its own form. When you have reached that point, what you do is to focus on its energy type. Meditate on it, feel it, experience it, know it. Allow yourself to sink deeper and deeper into it, until you identify with it so much that it starts to feel like your own. This sense of possession of the energy and it being yours is what you need to focus on as much as possible, until you are totally certain that it is, for the time being, your energy.

Having established this sense of owning that energy, refocus on the sense of the spirit form; it too is your form, for now. See how your new form is expressing the fundamental underlying characteristics of the energy you have taken on as yours. At this point, you should use the ᛇ Jór (Eihwaz) rune, chant its name and allow the radiating power of its deep violet energy to carry you forward. You will now become aware of the other awareness in the spirit form. Allow it to take the driving seat ask it to show you its own native realms that you would like to temporarily visit, and experience it as the spirit does, and let go. You need to allow the passive submissive side of you take hold; you are experiencing and learning, not doing. Let the awareness of the spirit drive all the interactions, all the active parts of the experience. The only interference you could present is by directing it with intent and desire, when there is something or someone in particular you would like it to look into more. Remember, it is only a suggestion: the spirit is in the driving seat, not you. Respect those boundaries at any cost. This establishes hard boundaries and observances to rules in the both of you. You will need those firmly in place, to the point where they are unchangeable, before doing any of the more advanced practices, both to protect you and the spirit, and to avoid possession as well as losing the Self within it. Such boundaries become very effective, actually essential, later on during advanced practices when it is the passive observer and you are the active party when merged.

Do this type of exploration with it in the driving seat a few times. Once this has become somewhat more familiar, you can start by taking the driving seat for a change. If you have established those rules just mentioned, the spirit will stay in the background without interfering when you are in control. Do not be afraid to ask it for suggestions when dealing with the unfamiliar; it is in its interest to avoid harm coming to you and to its spirit form! Remember that the intent with this type of experiencing is that you are going to temporarily visit and act in its realm or reality. See the subtle change? Good.

Allowing the Spirit to Experience Through Your Body

This is probably one of the most dangerous and advanced practices you can engage in with a spirit. The risk of possession is extremely high when doing this and it should only ever be done with spirits you are very comfortable with, whom you know intimately and with whom you have a good rules and protocols established so firmly that countering it is an unthinkable thing to both you and the spirit you are working with. It is best enforced with universal intent; your intent has to be precise, clear and unwavering. Do not take this warning lightly. From a personal point of view, I would personally strongly recommend never doing this. These are deeper practices of Seiðr and not something which should be engaged in for fun or amusement. Instead, their goal is spiritual growth – both yours and that of the spirit you are working with.

One thing which you need to keep in mind is that if you have not had a lot of practice with the given spirit, various parts of your Self will see its energy as totally alien and will instinctively strike out against it. This is a survival mechanism and, as such, cannot be countered per se. Instead, by regular practice, we acclimatise the Self and its constituent parts. This causes it to see the energy and spirit as familiar, and hopefully with all the positive experiences you will have gained when merging with the spirit form, some parts of the Self will echo positively with it. In turn, this causes a type of response which we can intellectualise as being equivalent to curiosity rise in the other parts of the Self. Curiosity is far more welcoming than an overt, aggressive 'stay away' type of response and this type of working starts to become possible. This is why intimacy and familiarity of the utmost degree is needed in between a Seiðr practitioner and their spirits.

This is a phased practice; in other words, we start from the least intense and overwhelming parts and build up. Avoid at all costs skipping part to get to whatever it is you may deem exciting. That is a recipe for disaster – in most cases literally disastrous!

By this stage being in each other's auric energy fields should be totally natural and effortless. What you are going to start by doing is the energy bathing practice given above, but this time, with the intent that the spirit's energy pulsates through your energy field until you intend it to stop. This is maintained initially for one hour, then three hours, then six hours and finally, 12 hours. At no time during this should you fall asleep. All you will be doing is your usual routines: work, going out and about and so forth. You will be avoiding any practice or relaxation which could potentially send you to sleep. Falling asleep during this can be dangerous. One, it allows the spirit to run riot within you and two, it also allows parts of your Self to go back into defensive sticking mode. This is its natural mode of functioning when not under the control of conscious awareness. Either of these situations can be dangerous at best and most certainly will cause massive problems for the development of further practices. For instance, if you have a rebelling Self which sees the spirit you are working with as an enemy, then you will at best have to work both against the spirit and your Self. In other words, you might as well give up completely. This is what we want to avoid. Take it slow, follow the instructions and do not deviate from your steps.

If you do need to stop or sleep, unwind your energies from the spirit and re-establish both your boundaries before doing so. There is no harm in stopping early whatsoever, do not hesitate in doing so, if circumstances demand it. The other thing to keep in mind is that your auric field will be a mix of the spirit's energy and your energy field. This might seem as a non-issue, but how you interact with the world at large, how people see and react to you and how the energy reality does will change in subtle and significant ways. You will also be visible from other realities (mainly those of the spirit's native realm), whereas before, you would not have been even noticed by them. You are, in this state of being, walking through the veil separating realities and taking a step in, out, back in, back out and so forth. You belong to both and hence can be influenced by both. Be cautious and take it slow, and for goodness' sake, be alert!

The next stage (assuming you have mastered the 12 hours perfectly) is to do what you would typically do with your personified Hamingja[11]. You are not only going to merge your energy fields but also intend the spirit to expand a little (if needed) and spill over your Lik, so that it is in effect containing your body. This is exactly the same as your personified Hamingja containing your

Lik, except now it is a spirit form. This will teach you to move with it, both within the Self and without it. Intend it to remain so, mimicking all the movements and actions you undertake, until you tell it to stop (never forget that condition at the end – the until is critically important in these practices). Then allow your sense of feeling to expand out a little beyond your skin, in order to encompass the spirit form. Try to keep this up for one hour, then three hours and then increase by three, until you reach 12 hours without too much effort. Then you need to stop – just intend the spirit to remain where it is and walk out of it. In effect, you and your body, with all other parts of the Self it contains, are walking out of the spirit form. As you move further away, the energy fields will also disentangle automatically.

These stages will suffice for the initial experiences with this practice. During this overlapping practice, the spirit will experience all you do in life. How you react to experiences will send off energy triggers and echoes within its own form, thereby effecting it too. So be careful: if you react with an intense emotion, it will experience a massive energy rush, which can send it into overdrive. Be very aware, that when using this method even pain is experienced by the spirit directly. Spirits react to pain very differently to how we humans do. Keep a close eye on all the impulses, thoughts and drives which flow through you when merged with a spirit in this way. Here, control is the key, but since you will have worked through initial training, this should not be an issue. If you have not done so, it is definitely time to do it before you undertake these practices.

Spirit Sex

It is best to deal with this before millions of queries start flooding in about it. Yes, sex is possible with spirits. Not only is it possible, but in Seiðr work, it represents a fundamental set of practices and training. It is a rather complex field to cover because due to the nature of these practices, the ways in which the women and men do them is very different; there are even two separate versions for the men where they act in a dually-sexual manner, for men are both. The penis and the prostate gland function as the two primary organs and energy organs in these mysteries. We will look at all these in later publications.

Rather than end things here, let us look at a quick rundown on the receptive side of such practices, since both genders can be receptive sexually. Sex with spirits, once it is achieved, can be extremely intense and addictive, and it will very quickly overshadow sex with another human being. The breadth of experience just simply far outweighs what can be done with an ordinary human being.

Let us keep the spirit energy gender to include both, but do remember, if you are a man, you are only to work with male spirits, otherwise you will suffer an energetic loss when the female spirit absorbs your masculine energy. There are no exceptions, no work-arounds and no ways to counter this. It is an energetic natural law and was one of the key reasons why Seiðr was not as a general rule taught to men. Such energy loss results in loss of power, abilities, draining of the Hamingja, Ørlǫg and eventually ancestral lines. Physically, fatigue, illness and premature aging take place, as well as the diminishing of masculinity. The more obsessively this is pursued, the more addictive it becomes and the more damaging. Remember, energy is already at an all-time low for human beings; we spend a very long time rebuilding those stores to normal levels even before we can afford the luxury of taking our initial steps on the spiritual (and mystic's) path. Losing even the smallest fraction is too much. Those who heed this warning will be the wise ones, and those who ignore it are the fools who will slow down until spiritual stasis kicks in, which will then, gradually but certainly, lead to energetic (and hence physical) stasis.

The great advantage of spirits is that they can, once in spirit form, reach every nerve of our bodies as and when they are allowed to, and sometimes some will not even bother to be 'allowed', those are the types of spirits to be avoided in the first place. Due to this and for both women and men, spirits can reach parts of our physiology through the Hamr which is difficult, if not impossible, to reach for a human partner. For instance, in the case of men, for a spirit form to sink its hand through your body and directly grab hold of the prostate gland (the male g-spot, in case anyone is still ignorant of that fact) and stimulate it in ways in which no human being ever could is very easy. Most men do not even know what basic feeling of the prostate gland is like, unless they have had to undergo a medical exam. The same ease of reach for a spirit can be said for women's g-spots. It is not only limited to actual g-spots and organs, but every nerve, every sensory tissue, every energy channel in the bodies – they are all exposed and readily available to manipulation by the spirit. Actually, the equivalent to Kundalini practices are to be found in these practices (Seiðr sexual), but more on that at a later time, in its own dedicated book.

With the proper spirit sexual partner, both men and women can enter into deep states of sexual trances, leading to sexually fuelled states of ecstasy. At their peak, the physiology is taken to the point of extreme overdrive, where our biology becomes overclocked, during which the biological awareness itself separates from its physical components and takes conscious awareness along for the ride with it. This is why death and ecstasy states are so interlinked. It is not because death is sexual, as some profess it to be – that is nothing more than a side effect of mental association of the two experiences/beliefs. The reason they are associated is because once awoken, the biological awareness separates from its host the Lik. Upon death it unifies the rest of the Self. It is exactly the same effect we experience during sexual ecstatic trances at their peak. The only difference is that with the former, it is permanent and the latter, is temporary; with the former, you need no help, as it happens no matter what (providing of course that you have actually awoken the Self), whereas with the latter, you need a spirit to work with and/or an actual human partner.

A quick starter practice can be outlined at this point. Men make sure you keep your hands away from your genitals! NO touching. Women should do the same for this practice. Make sure you have a well-established spirit form for the spirit you intend to work with. Naturally, doing this with a sexual spirit is ideal; others will have to be taught, whilst some simply have no inclination towards it whatsoever. Water spirits are best for the deep emotional type of sexual exchange and ideal for women, while for men, fire spirits of an explosive nature are ideal. As it turns out, those specific elemental characteristics match the spiritual energetic genders too; the vast majority of water spirits are female and practically all fire spirits are male. They match the gender sexual inclinations too: water spirits will cling to you and like to make you feel good, their sexual interactions are gentle and slowly arousing, building up the momentum over time, while fire spirits match the masculine sexual mind-set perfectly, and they are aggressive, quick to action and pushy, they will flare you up in no time, and will push and force you into whatever ecstasy is needed or desired with such force that you will not be able to even follow until you are done. Because they are fire-based, male spirits will hyper-energise you; unlike when having sex with a human partner, if you are male, you would be tired afterwards, but with a fire-based sexual spirit, you will feel totally invigorated. It literally can be described as a feeling of being on top of the world. They are highly transformative and as you release your lower, more physical type of energy, which you produce during sex, they will consume it to fuel themselves and as a result of that process, they explode outwards, flooding you with their own as it pours out of them. Their energy will quicken and heighten every part of your Self. This is a good example of the higher level of energisation women experience when they have sex with human male partners. Now you too will have that glow about you, which people are so quick to pick up on from women when they have had sex.

All you need to do to initiate a sexual encounter with a so inclined spirit is to lie down with as little clothing on as possible and relax. Use the practices given above to link up energetically with the spirit and intend to have sex with it. Intend it to touch, intend it to awaken your energy structures, intend them to carry you into sexual ecstasy. If need be, use the same techniques you used when you were in the spirit's form and you were prompting them to view or enquire more from the background in their own form (remember when you were visiting its realm and it was in the driving seat!). Use the same passive submissive promptings. Men will start feeling an erection build up. Whatever you do, leave it alone – you are not supposed to touch or stimulate anything; that is what the spirit is going to be doing. If you struggle with self-control during arousal, get some help. Be creative (and be safe!). NO touching allowed. Well, not by human hands, in any case. Let the spirit do what it needs to do and relax. Your body will eventually start to shift, pulses of sexual fires will burn through you, you will feel the probing and flow of hands, and you will eventually start to experience orgasmic reactions coursing through your body randomly and undirected. Allow it all to pass. Your penis will start to have larger and larger quantities of pre-cum flowing. We will cover what to do with that at a later time. Just ignore it for now. Allow this sexual orgasmic pulsing to intensify as much as it can. Most men will eventually ejaculate automatically, whether they want to or not. That is fine. Offer the energetic and substance within that to the spirit you have been working with. This will amplify its physicality and energy, as well as reinforce and strengthen the bond in between you. And relax, avoid ejaculation and allow things to reach a peak and come to an end. You will still feel all energised and wanting more, but your physical body will just be too exhausted to keep on going. Respect your body. As its biological awareness grows, so will its skills and capabilities in these practices.

For women, they will experience something very similar, although the multiple orgasms will be less intense but more regular, gradually building up in tempo and rhythm. These reactions are far more natural for women than men. Men have to learn it, while women have it in their vast inherited experiential knowledge pools. It is rather ironic that women were fighting for their sexual freedom of expression, when in fact men are the oppressed ones who need to learn from practically the basics onwards.

Once you have started having sexual experiences with the spirit, it is important to understand that it can – and most often will – re-initiate them, whenever it gets the opportunity. You have two ways of dealing with this; if you are not in company, just accept them. It would be utterly mad to reject them, as when they are initiated by the spirit itself, it is with the intent to take you to a new height which was not possible previously. Secondly, it is important to remember that in these practices, you are the respondent, not the initiator. Always keep this in mind before venturing into them for the first time. That is the only time you have any actual choice; you either choose to get involved in this type of practice or you do not, with the full knowledge that once you do, you do so in perfect understanding that the spirit will always have the say on when and how the next interaction is initiated. Refusing it is only an option at the first occurrence. The laws of intent dictate that once the intent to experience sexual encounters with a given spirit is given, it is given and unleashed. There is no thing such as un-intending. YOU HAVE BEEN WARNED. What it does not mean is that you will only ever have sex with this given spirit – or spirits, for that matter. What it does mean is that when the spirit decides it wants to have sex, you have no choice but to go with the flow. Remember, that is the fundamental of such practices. If you are uncertain, even to the slightest degree, do not even try it; that first time is all it takes to unravel an entire set of new Ørlög. There is no point complaining later on about a spirit forcing itself on you sexually, there simply is no such thing, as human social norms do not apply. Once you say 'yes', it is 'yes', no matter whether you meant 'no' or 'not now' – all those things are irrelevant. And just to avoid confusion, a 'yes' is a 'yes' for as long as you are alive, and in some cases, such as with water spirits, a 'yes' even carries on after death across the ancestral lines. The best outcome in those situations you can hope for is years and years of struggling to try and push the spirit away, which would be catastrophic for your own spiritual development. So if there is even the smallest tiniest doubt, just stay away from sexual practices with spirits.

If these sexual experiences are not welcome when it makes the advances, just enjoy its touch and explain to it that you are around people or in a situation where you cannot get privacy or are simply not interested. Also, let it know that you will be happy to take it up on its offer later on that day/evening, when you are alone. Practically all spirits accept that as a given fact when dealing with humans. Just as well most spirits will know when it is not appropriate, because for you to be at the point where they have spirit form and you are very familiar with them, they will be there in view of your actions and know that you lack privacy. What they might do is speed things up so that whatever you are doing ends quickly, so that you are no longer busy!

As previously noted, these are good introductory practices. Sexual Seiðr is a highly complex and intricate field of practice in its own right, requiring a fundamental level of skill and patience. We will look at some of its other methods in due course.

Merging of Hvels

Not everyone will be familiar with the term Hvel; those are wheels, energetic ones. A similar concept is found abound in modern-day new age literature, where the term 'chakra' is used instead. Imported from the Eastern traditions, the concept of the chakra is very similar to the Hvel (which translated to wheel) with only a few differences:

1. The Norse Hvel do not have deities/gods/goddesses associated with the Hvels. In our tradition, guardians that hold our hands on our journey are not needed. Actually, the very concept is insulting to the Norse-minded because our tradition is that of the warriors, where action and pushing ahead no matter what, and battling the obstacles and growing as a result of our experiences is the driving force. We are not the child who needs a parenting guide or chaperone ; we find our own ways or become lost in stasis and the Gap.
2. We do not have runes associated with each Hvel.
3. Even though many would like it so, we do not have the Nine Worlds associated with a specific Hvels. All forces in Midgard as a central point of creation are a mix of more or less of the Nine

Worlds, hence assigning a given specific world to a Hvel would deny it the complete flow it naturally receives. Some of the primary Hvel do have energies of a world as the domiant one but not the sole energy type. For instance, Múspellsheim energy is the primary one for the large Hvel under our feet but it is not ONLY Múspellsheim's energy type there.

4. What they do have is elemental connotations, which represent the density and activity of the forces which enter our beings.

5. We have a very different number of Hvels and slightly different linking positions.

6. We have Hvels which are physical and act as distribution centres for physically generated energy (the dense energies, if you like), and we have Hvels within the Hamr which distribute energies at a slightly subtler layer to which the Hamr belongs.

7. Our Hvel distribution is very different to that of the Eastern system; these differences are inherently based on the fact that not only is our physiology and DNA different but so are our Hamr.

8. We have Nine Hvels in the Hamr, with another nine outside of it. Women have six Hvels in their physical bodies (the lucky ones!) whilst men have five. The additional one for women is a massive perceptual Hvel which gives them their natural highly proficient energy-sensing abilities. How unfair!

9. Our Hvel structures are optimised according to genetics, and even though we can learn the general patterns, each race will have inherent differences and optimisations which the others will not. Each is optimised for their specific bio-energy systems and they are not really compatible across each

other – just as the Hvels are not at all compatible with their Eastern equivalents (chakras).

When it comes to working with spirits, the Hvels can be used to great advantage. Sexually, by merging our Hvels with the spirits' energy flows, states of mind which can be thought of as extreme forms of ecstasy can be achieved. By channelling spirit energy through the Hvels in specific ways, we can materialise the spirit forms and channel their powers through our bodies, and by merging the spirit energies with the Hvels during the spirit mead production within our own Óðrerir, we can produce a unique type of mead, which depending on the spirit, can produce a whole range of different effects and abilities. This is what we could term runic alchemy at its highest form of practice. We will look at all these in due course.

For the time being, if you are of Indo-European heritage, you can use the following Hvel boosts in your spirit sex practices. On the back at the mid-back level, and on the front left and right (think liver and pancreas level) are a total of three physiological Hvels. If, during sex, you drive the incoming energy from the spirit into those, it will result in increased vitality. If you drive the energy into the Hamr Hvel at the base of your feet, it will stir the brilliance slumbering there and activate enhanced awareness. For the adventurous few, in men, in between your legs (inner thighs), just where the genitals rest when you are sitting with legs touching, you will find there, on the left inner leg and the right (just sit hold your knees together where you feel them squeezing your testicles), are two separate mini-Hvels in Hamr when, during sex, you force the energy to flow there (by shifting your awareness and focussing on them), it will amplify ALL the sexual energy and the intensity of that energy. For men, the prostate gland also acts as a quasi-Hvel, and any energy you force there by focus and intent to absorb will trigger multiple micro-orgasms AND transform the energy to whatever type your body needs. With practice, you can force it to transform it into any type of familiar energy type.

For women, a great trick is to force the sexual energy deep into the Hvel within the womb in the physical). Since this is the Hvel of extra-sensory perception, it will not only boost your perceptive abilities but will trigger direct energy perception. For the ladies with a natural ability for Spa foresight, it will trigger flashes of foresight when awoken. Unfortunately, men do not have an equivalent Hvel to achieve the same effects.

We will look at the inner working of the Hvels at a later time, for they hold much to discovered and much to be avoided! These few words are sufficient to allow the adventurous to experiment a little and trigger a few nice and safe effects, without being too creative and causing harm.

This brings us to the end of this book. I do hope it gives you a good solid starting point and some exciting practices to work on. There will be an advanced book which picks up from here and delves into far more complex practices which build on the skills and foundations you will have established here.

Notes from the publisher: the original manuscript included an additional chapter on spirit infusers, how to craft and use them. It was meant as an introduction to the advanced practices of spirit walking. We have decided to remove it. It will be published at a later time in the title dealing with advanced spirit walking. This was simply due to the requirement of skills which are not covered in these chapters and would have left readers with significant gaps of knowledge when it came to their crafting and use.

APPENDIXES

APPENDIX A

Table of Runic Names in Icelandic & Germanic

Rune	Numeric Value	Icelandic Name	Germanic Name
ᚠ	1	Fé	Fehu
ᚢ	2	Úr	Uruz
ᚦ	3	Þurs	Thurisaz
ᚨ	4	Óss (Ás)	Ansuz
ᚱ	5	Reið	Raidho
ᚲ	6	Kaun	Kenaz
ᚷ	7	Gjöf	Gebo
ᚹ	8	Vin	Wunjo
ᚺ	9	Hagall	Hagalaz
ᚾ	10	Nauð	Nauthiz
ᛁ	11	Íss	Isa
ᛃ	12	Ár	Jera
ᛇ	13	Perð	Pertho
ᛈ	14	Jór	Eihwaz
ᛉ	15	Ýr	Elhaz
ᛋ	16	Sól	Sowilo
ᛏ	17	Týr	Tiwaz
ᛒ	18	Bjarkan	Berkano
ᛖ	19	Eykur	Ehwaz
ᛗ	20	Maður	Mannaz
ᛚ	21	Lögur	Laguz
ᛜ	22	Ing	Ingwaz
ᛞ	23	Dagur	Dagaz
ᛟ	24	Óðal	Othala

APPENDIX B

References & footnotes

1. Strange Footprints on the Land (Author: Irwin, Constance publisher: Harper & Row, 1980) ISBN 0-06-022772-9)

2. Snorri Sturluson. The Prose Edda: Tales from Norse Mythology, translated by Jean I. Young (University of California Press, 1964)

3. Snorri Sturluson, Ynglinga Saga, Heimskringla, chapter 4

4. Hyndluljóð, Stanza 5, st. Poetic Edda & Gylfaginning

5. Völuspá - Stanza 1 (source: http://www.voluspa.org/literal/voluspa.htm)

6. Völuspá - Stanza 2 (source: http://www.voluspa.org/literal/voluspa.htm)

7. Deikman, A. J. (1982). "The Observing Self: Mysticism and Psychotherapy.", Boston: Beacon Press. ISBN 0-8070-2950-5, p. 21.

8. see what is known as the Icelandic Brennuöld (Age of Fire): 1654 where 20 people predominantly men were burnt at the stake (for more information on Icelandic history see: https://guidetoiceland.is/history-culture/history-of-iceland/ or/witchcraft-in-iceland).

9. Frank A. Rúnaldrar (2017), "The Spirit of Húnir Awakens - Part 1", London: Bastian & West, ISBN: 978-0-9955343-2-2, 'Focal Lens of Awareness' p.93

10. Frank A. Rúnaldrar (2017), "The Breath of Oðin Awakens", London: Bastian & West, ISBN: 978-0-9955343-4-6,

'Awakening the Breath of Oðin', p.77, the portion where you descend into the core of yourself.

11. ante.

FORTHCOMING TITLES

High Galdr: Rune Science
The Ultimate Book of Runes

Runes, runes and more runes! The sacred science of the Gods, the runes were made available to their children, our Ancestors. Much information is available about the runes, yet so very little is known as to how they are actually used. They are chanted, they are written, and they are drawn. Yet all these methods fail to produce rapid or tangible manifestations.

Using the runes is a science and, like any science, the rules under which its principles operate need to be known. Unleashing a runic vocalisation using proper Galdr has been kept secret for ages, known to only an extremely select few who were capable of mastering their very Self. These methods for Galdr were passed down through generations as part of our vocal tradition, with only sparse written instruction preserved.

At long last, actual methods and underlying principles of manifesting the power of the runes are being made available unabridged with no hidden facets, no secret methods left unturned. Learn at long last how to wield the runes, how to unleash and manifest them, how to recode reality and reform events in life using the heritage left to us by our Ancestors and living with-in our DNA. Each and every rune holds a secret, a key, a power, a source of knowledge and a potential.

Learn to unleash it ALL with actual High Galdr.

DreamWalking
The Art of Runic Dreaming

Dreaming, everyone does it, yet not everyone remembers it, some like it others fear it but no one can agree on what dreaming actually is and why we all dream. Science argues it is a result of the brain consolidating daily information and memories, Psychology argues it is a reflection of the inner state of being and mental balance, mystics argue it is a separation of the spirit from the body and so forth.

In Runic dreaming we explore and learn how to both use dreams and grow through them. Combining High Galdr with the Arts of the Völva (Old Norse Prophetess or Seeress) the full power of dreaming is unleashed as a transformation or awakening tool, an essential in reclaiming the full power of human awareness as it takes its first steps across creation.

Learn about runic energy and its impact on dreams, how to remember your dreams and use memory as a gauge of development, how to imbue the Minni (memory) to enhance dream capabilities, how to increase energy via dreams, how to experience the other Nine Worlds through dreams and how to bridge the dream and daily realities to shape the one through the other and vice versa...

www.ingramcontent.com/pod-product-compliance
Lightning Source LLC
Chambersburg PA
CBHW022103160426
43198CB00008B/332